Classic

Chicken

Recipes

Classic

Chicken

Recipes

Sue Ashworth

Jacqueline Bellefontaine

Jennie Berresford

Joanna Craig

Jill Eggleton

Nicola Fowler

Carole Handslip

Jane Hartshorn

Kathryn Hawkins

Cara Hobday

Deh-ta Hsiung

Wendy Lee

Louise Steele

Rosemary Wadey

Pamela Westland

SMITHMARK

This edition published in 1998 by SMITHMARK Publishers,
a division of U.S. Media Holdings Inc.,
115 West 18th Street, New york, NY 10011.

SMITHMARK books are available for bulk purchase for sales promotion and premium
use. For details write or call the manager of special sales, SMITHMARK Publishers,
115 West 18th Street, New York, NY 10011.

Edited, designed and produced by Haldane Mason, London

Acknowledgments
Editor: Anne Hildyard
Design: dap ltd
Photographer: St John Asprey (for pages 22, 23–24, 26–31, 33–36, 40, 59–65,
66–73, 78–80, 81–82, 83–86, 87–97, 98, 101–101, 118–125, 127–133, 145, 146–149, 150–155,
156–165, 172–176, 177–185, 186–187, 206–219, 221, 236–247, 248–251)
Home Economist: Jacqueline Bellefontaine (*for above pages*)
Other Photography: Karl Adamson, Sue Atkinson, Iain Bagwell, Martin Brigdale,
Amanda Heywood, Joff Lee, Patrick McLeavey, Clive Streeter
Home Economists: Sue Ashworth, Jennie Berresford, Joanna Craig, Jill Eggleton,
Nicola Fowler, Carole Handslip, Jane Hartshorn, Kathryn Hawkins, Cara Hobday,
Deh-ta Hsiung, Wendy Lee, Louise Steele, Rosemary Wadey, Pamela Westland

The publishers would like to thank the British Chicken Information Service for providing
the recipes on pages 22, 40, 59–65, 81–82, 87–97, 100–101, 127–133, 146–149,
156–165, 172–176, 186–187, 206–219, 221, 236–247.

Recipes on the following pages courtesy of Tom Bridge: 23–24, 26–31, 33–36,
66–73, 78–80, 83–86, 98, 118–125, 145, 150–155, 177–185, 248–251

The publishers would like to thank Divertimenti for kindly loaning them equipment
for the following pages: 64, 80, 82, 87, 89, 91, 101, 124, 128, 129, 130, 145,
159, 160, 161, 173, 213, 216, 217, 218, 236, 241

ISBN: 0-7651-0878-X

Printed in Italy

10 9 8 7 6 5 4 3 2 1

Note
Cup measurements in this book are for American cups.
Tablespoons are assumed to be 15 ml. Unless otherwise stated, milk is assumed to be
full-fat, eggs are medium and pepper is freshly ground black pepper.

Contents

Pies, Pastries, & Terrines 166

Barbecues & Broils 188

Hot & Spicy 222

Index 252

Introduction

Chicken has become justly popular around the whole world and plays an important part in the modern diet, being reasonably priced and nutritionally sound. It was not always the case, at one time only the affluent could afford to eat chicken. It was not until after World War II, when modern production methods started, that chicken became more plentiful and cheaper, enabling everyone to take advantage of a low-cost, healthy food.

Chicken is a versatile meat that lends itself to an enormous range of recipes, cooking methods, and cuisines. Its unassertive flavor means that it is equally suited to cooking with herbs, spices, fruit, vegetables, and sweet and savory flavors. Because it has a low fat content, especially without the skin, it is an ideal meat for low cholesterol and calorie-controlled diets—3½ ounces of white meat contains only 4 grams of fat. If you want to reduce fat further, cooking methods that require little added fat include poaching, broiling, roasting, or stir-frying. The skin can be left on during cooking to keep the meat moist and then removed before serving to reduce the fat content. As well as being an excellent source of protein, chicken contains valuable minerals, such as potassium and phosphorus, and some of the B vitamins.

There are many different types of chicken available. Whole birds come as broilers or roasters, boilers, which are older birds that need longer cooking, and small baby chickens, known as Rock Cornish hens. Broilers are also sold jointed into portions. Further options to choose from concern feeding and rearing methods. These include corn-fed chickens, free-range chickens that are not reared intensively but are free to roam in a traditional farmyard, and Poulet de Bresse, a French breed that is larger than normal.

The recipes in this book encompass several cooking methods and are gathered from many different cuisines. Choose from soups, starters, snacks and salads, roasts and bakes, casseroles, quick chicken dishes, pies, pastries, and terrines, barbecues and broils, and hot and spicy dishes. As well as all the classic dishes, there are creative, contemporary recipes with some surprising twists. Whatever the occasion, the perfect dish is guaranteed to be found in this book.

Buying Guide

When buying fresh chicken, always check the sell-by date and make sure that the chicken feels chilled. Look for chicken that is undamaged, with no dark patches and few traces of feathers. Check the smell, which should be clean and fresh. Remove any giblets and store these separately. The flesh should feel soft and flexible and give slightly when pressed.

CHOOSING A CHICKEN

Baby chicken Also known as poussin or Rock Cornish hen, these are 4–6-week old birds weighing between 12–20 ounces. One whole bird is usually needed for each person. Because they are so young and have not developed a lot of flavor, flavor must be added in the form of stuffing or a marinade.

Boiling fowl These are large birds over 10 months old, with a good flavor. They are ideal for casseroles or for making stock, but are generally too tough for roasting or broiling.

Broiler or frying chicken These birds are reared to produce tender flesh, and are usually 6–8 weeks old, weighing 3–4 pounds. They are best used jointed and broiled or fried, but whole birds can also be roasted, steamed, or casseroled.

Capon These are large, castrated cockerels, about 10 weeks old, and can weigh as much as 10 pounds. They have a greater proportion of white meat and the flesh is delicately marbled with fat which gives it an excellent flavor. These are becoming increasingly uncommon and in some countries it is now illegal for farmers to raise them.

Corn-fed chicken These are reared on a diet containing large amounts of corn, a food often used in south-west France. The corn is thought to give a good flavor and the skin of these birds is a distinctive yellow color. They usually weigh between 3–5 pounds.

Free-range chicken These have the freedom to feed at will and the space to run free, either in large, airy barns or in the farmyard. Barn-reared birds are slaughtered at 8–10 weeks, and farmyard birds at 1–12 weeks. They have a bigger, broader shape than the factory-reared broiler or roaster, and usually have a better flavor.

Poulet de Bresse Reared in the Burgundy region of France, these birds are fed on natural, high-quality food in free-range conditions. Perhaps because of this, their flavor is believed to be superior and this is reflected in their price.

Roaster These weigh about 4–8 pounds and are about 10 weeks old when slaughtered. They are best roasted whole, but if they are not too large, they can be jointed and used for frying or broiling. One roaster is usually sufficient to feed a family.

Spring chicken Also known as a double poussin, this is a 9–12-week-old bird, weighing about 2½ pounds, which is large enough to feed two people.

Chicken Cuts

When you do not require a whole chicken, various choices of chicken cuts are available ready-packaged. Using cuts means quicker cooking and no wastage. There are choices of preparation as some chicken pieces are skinless and boneless, while others have both bone and skin. Of course, the more preparation that is done, the more expensive the cut will be.

Breast
Chicken breasts are available with or without skin, and either boneless or with the bone left in. The white meat is lean and succulent and can be simply cooked in butter or oil, or stuffed to add extra flavor.

Leg
The leg can be easily separated into a drumstick and thigh. If left as one piece, a large cut such as this is best cooked slowly—poached or casseroled—rather than broiled or fried.

Drumstick
This cut is convenient to eat at barbecues or buffet meals as it can be picked up easily. It is ideal for frying or barbecuing and can be first marinated or coated in bread crumbs.

Thigh
Any slow-cooking method is suitable for this cut, and it is good used in recipes for casseroles and stews. The meat on thighs is dark but it is very succulent and juicy. Skinless boneless thighs are ideal for stuffing and rolling.

Wing
Although not very meaty, many people enjoy this cut when fried or roasted. If the wing tips are cut off, wings are a good candidate for the barbecue.

Ground chicken
Where a mild flavor is preferred, ground chicken makes a good substitute for ground red meat. It is also useful to make patties, rissoles, and sausages.

Chicken liver
This is found either in the freezer or delicatessen. It is very tasty in rice dishes and can be used to make pâtés or cooked and tossed over warm salads.

Preparation Techniques

There are a number of different ways of preparing a whole chicken for cooking. The following techniques will help to make carving easier, speed up cooking times, and even help to save you some money!

Butterflying

The butterflying technique involves flattening the bird so that it can be cooked more quickly. This method is ideal for broiling or barbecuing.

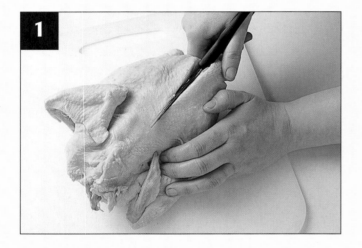

1 Put the chicken on a chopping board with the breast downward. Cut through the bottom part of the carcass using poultry shears or heavy kitchen scissors, making sure not to cut right through to the breast bone below.

2 Rinse the chicken with cold water, drain and place on a board with the skin side uppermost. Press the chicken flat, then cut off the leg ends. Thread two long wooden skewers through the bird to keep it flat.

Cutting up a Chicken

Cutting up a chicken yourself is a cheaper option than buying ready-prepared portions and you can choose whether to cut the chicken into four or eight portions. Use either poultry shears or a sharp knife and strong kitchen scissors. First remove the legs: use a sharp knife and cut through the skin where the leg is attached to the body. Hold the leg away from the body and twist to break the ball and socket joint. Cut through the joint and remove the leg. Remove the other leg in the same way. Separate the breast from the back-bone, cut through the flap of skin below the rib cage and cut toward the neck. Pull the breast and back apart and cut through the joints that connect them. Take one side of the breast in each hand and hold skin side down. Bend each side until the breastbone becomes free. Remove it with your fingers and a knife. Cut the breast in half through the wishbone. Now cut each breast in half so that some is included with each wing. Finally, separate the thigh and drumstick.

Boning a Chicken

To make carving simpler, it is necessary to bone a chicken. Use a sharp knife with a
short blade and keep the knife against the bone, using short, scraping actions.

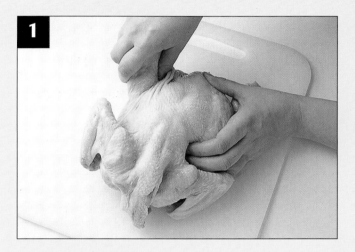

1 Dislocate each leg by breaking it at the thigh joint. Carefully remove the wishbone with a small knife.

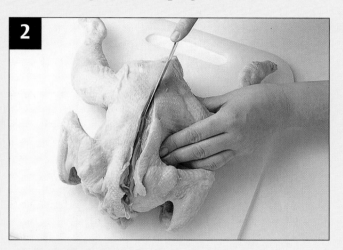

2 With the bird breast-side down on a chopping board, cut down the center of the backbone from the neck to the tail end.

3 Working from the front to the back, scrape away the flesh on one side of the backbone, cutting into the bird to expose the rib cage.

4 Repeat on the other side, being careful not to pierce the breast skin with the knife. Pull the rib and backbone from the flesh of the bird.

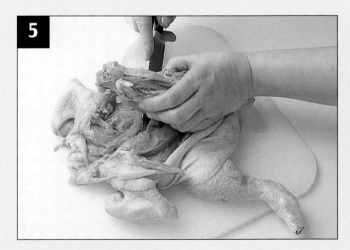

5 Scrape away the flesh from each thigh bone and cut away the bone at the joint with a small knife or poultry shears. Scrape all the flesh away from the wings up to the first joint.

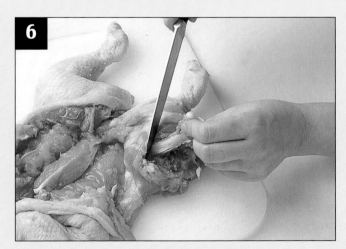

6 Remove the exposed wing bone by cutting away the rest of the wing at the joint. Cut away the tendon from each fillet and breast. The chicken is now ready for stuffing and rolling.

Cooking Methods for Chicken

All types of chicken can be roasted, from baby chickens to larger birds.
With crisp, golden-brown skin and moist, succulent meat,
a perfectly roasted chicken is always popular.

ROASTING

Before roasting, remove any fat from the body cavity. Rinse the bird inside and out with water, then pat dry with paper towels. Season the cavity generously with salt and pepper and add stuffing, herbs, or lemon if desired. Spread the breast of the chicken with softened butter or oil. Set on a rack in a roasting pan or shallow ovenproof dish. Roast the bird, and baste two or three times with the pan juices during roasting.

Alternatively, cover the chicken with a piece of cheesecloth that has been dipped in melted butter and there is no need to baste. If the chicken is browning too quickly, cover it with foil. Test to check if it is done by using a meat thermometer or insert the point of a sharp knife into the thickest part of the thigh. If the chicken is cooked, the juices will run clear with no trace of pink. Put the bird on a carving board and let rest for at least 15 minutes before serving. Make a sauce or gravy from the juices left in the roasting pan.

Carving a Chicken

1 Grasp the leg and move it outward from the body. Using a sharp knife, cut each drumstick and thigh from the body, then cut through the joint to separate the drumstick and thigh.

2 Make a deep horizontal cut just above the wing, through the breast, until the knife touches the breastbone.

3 Slice the breast thinly in a series of vertical cuts going down to the first horizontal cut.

CHICKEN ROASTING TIMES		
TYPE OF CHICKEN & TEMPERATURE	WEIGHT	COOKING TIME
Rock Cornish hen 350°F	1–1½ pounds	1–1¼ hours
Chicken 375°F	2½–3 pounds	1–1¼ hours
	3½–4 pounds	1¼–2 hours
	4½–5 pounds	1½–2 hours
	5–6 pounds	1¾–2¼ hours

BROILING

Broiling is a good way of cooking chicken. The intense heat of the broiler quickly seals the succulent flesh beneath a crisp, golden exterior. For the best results the chicken should be placed 4–6 inches away from a moderate heat source. If the chicken seems to be browning too quickly, turn down the heat slightly. If the chicken is broiled at too high a temperature too near to the heat, the outside will burn before the inside is cooked. If it is cooked for too long under a low heat, it will dry out. Rock Cornish hens, spring chickens, and small roasters are least likely to dry out and become tough.

So that it can brown and cook evenly, cut a whole chicken into portions. For small chickens, split the chicken on either side of the backbone and cut the backbone out, then with the bird breast-side up, press firmly on the breastbone to break it and flatten the breast. Fold the wing tips back and behind and thread a long metal skewer through one wing, then the breast, and out through the other wing. Thread another skewer through the thighs. This technique is commonly known as butterflying.

Chicken quarters are best reduced to smaller cuts. Divide leg portions into thighs and drumsticks. Breast meat, if cooked in one piece, can be rather dry and is best divided into bite-size chunks for kabobs, or sliced and pounded flat to make escalopes. Wings are perfect for speedy broiling—the bones disperse the heat and the skin traps moisture to make a wonderfully succulent, tasty dish.

BROILING TIMES FOR CHICKEN	
TYPE OF CHICKEN	COOKING TIME
Chicken portions	30–35 minutes
Skinless, boneless chicken breast	10–12 minutes
Spring chicken, butterflied	25–30 minutes
Rock Cornish hen, butterflied	20–25 minutes
Roasting chicken, halved or butterflied	30–40 minutes

Marinades

- **Chicken in Pita Bread** *(see page 54)*
- **Supreme of Chicken with Black Cherries** *(see page 83)*
- **Honeyed Citrus Chicken** *(see page 97)*
- **Golden Glazed Chicken** *(see page 159)*
- **Chicken in Spicy Yogurt** *(see page 192)*
- **Mediterranean Broiled Chicken** *(see page 194)*
- **Tandoori Chicken** *(see page 196)*
- **Jerk Chicken** *(see page 200)*
- **Thai Chicken with Peanut Sauce** *(see page 202)*
- **Sweet and Sour Drumsticks** *(see page 221)*

FRYING

This cooking method is suitable for small thighs, drumsticks, and cuts. To pan-fry, first dry the chicken pieces with kitchen paper so that they brown properly and to prevent spitting during cooking. If required, the chicken can be coated in seasoned flour, egg, and bread crumbs or a batter. Heat oil or a mixture of oil and butter in a heavy-based skillet. When the oil is very hot, add the chicken pieces, skin-side down. Fry until deep golden brown all over, turning the pieces frequently during cooking. The breast usually cooks before the drumsticks and thighs. Drain well on kitchen paper before serving.

SAUTÉING

This method is ideal for small pieces or small birds, such as baby chickens. It can combine braising, where the chicken is first sautéed, then cooked in stock or other liquid. Heat a little oil or a mixture of oil and butter in a heavy-based skillet. Add the chicken and fry over a moderate heat until golden brown, turning often during cooking to brown all over. Add stock or other liquid, bring to a boil, then cover, and reduce the heat. Cook gently until the chicken is cooked through.

STIR-FRYING

Skinless, boneless chicken is cut into pieces of equal size, either strips, small cubes or thin slices. This ensures that the meat cooks evenly and stays succulent. Preheat a wok or saucepan before adding a small amount of oil. When the oil starts to smoke, add the chicken pieces and stir-fry with your chosen flavorings for 3–4 minutes until cooked through. Other ingredients can be cooked at the same time, or the chicken can be cooked by itself, then removed from the pan while you stir-fry the remaining ingredients. Return the chicken to the pan briefly when the other ingredients are cooked.

CASSEROLING

Casseroling is a method that is good for cooking cuts from larger, more mature chickens, although smaller chickens can be cooked whole. The slow cooking produces tender meat with a good flavor. Brown the chicken in butter or hot oil or a mixture of both. Add some stock, wine, or a mixture of both with seasonings and herbs, cover, and cook on the hotplate or in the oven until the chicken is tender. Add a selection of lightly sautéed vegetables about halfway through the cooking time.

BRAISING

This method does not require liquid—the chicken pieces or a small whole chicken and vegetables are cooked together slowly in a low oven. Heat some oil in a flameproof casserole and gently fry the chicken until golden all over. Remove the chicken and fry a selection of vegetables until they are almost tender. Replace the chicken, cover tightly, and cook very gently on the hotplate or in a low oven until the chicken and vegetables are tender.

POACHING

Poaching is a gentle cooking method that produces tender chicken and a stock that can be used to make a sauce to serve with the chicken. Put a whole chicken, a bouquet garni, a leek, a carrot, and an onion in a large flameproof casserole. Cover with water, season, and bring to a boil. Cover and simmer for 1½–2 hours, until the chicken is tender. Lift the chicken out, discard the bouquet garni, and use the stock to make a sauce. The vegetables can be blended to thicken the stock and served with the chicken.

Food Safety & Tips

Chicken is liable to be contaminated by salmonella bacteria, which can cause severe food poisoning. When storing, handling. and preparing poultry, certain precautions must be observed to prevent the possibility of food poisoning.

- Check the sell-by date and best before date. After buying, take the chicken home quickly, preferably in a freezer bag or cool box.

- Return frozen birds immediately to the freezer.

- If storing in the refrigerator, remove the wrappings and store any giblets separately. Place the chicken in a shallow dish to catch drips. Cover loosely with foil and store on the bottom shelf of the refrigerator for no more than two or three days, depending on the best before date. Avoid any contact between raw chicken and cooked food during storage and preparation. Wash your hands after handling raw chicken.

- Prepare raw chicken on a chopping board that can be easily cleaned and bleached, such as a nonporous, plastic board.

- Check the temperature of the refrigerator regularly, it should not exceed 42°F.

- Frozen birds should be thawed before cooking. If time permits, thaw for about 36 hours in the refrigerator, or thaw for about 12 hours in a cool place. Bacteria breed in warm food at room temperature and when chicken is thawing. Cooking at high temperatures kills bacteria. There should be no ice crystals and the flesh should feel soft and flexible. Cook as soon as possible after thawing.

- Make sure that chicken is thoroughly cooked. Test to check it is done with a meat thermometer—the thigh should reach at least 175°F when cooked—or by piercing the thickest part of a thigh with the point of a sharp knife, the juices should run clear, not pink or red. Never partially cook chicken with the intention of completing cooking later. Bacteria multiply at an alarming rate in warm food, when optimum conditions prevail for the bacteria to increase.

Chicken Stock

Chicken stock is usually made from a whole bird or wings, backs, and legs. This makes a well-flavored stock. However it can also be made using chicken bones and carcass cooked with vegetables and flavorings. Although it will not be so rich in flavor, it is still superior to stock made from a bouillon cube. Homemade stock can be stored in the freezer for up to 6 months. A simple chicken stock can be made using the giblets (except the liver, which is bitter) with a bouquet garni, onion, carrot, and some peppercorns. Salt is not added as this concentrates in flavor as the stock reduces during cooking. Salt can be added to taste when the stock is used in soups and other dishes.

If a whole bird is used to make the stock, the meat can be used in soups and casseroles.

To make chicken stock: add the wings, backs, or whole chicken to a large pan with two quartered onions. Cook until the chicken and onion are evenly browned. Cover with cold water, bring to a boil, and skim off any scum that rises to the surface. Add two chopped carrots, two chopped celery stalks, a small bunch of parsley, a few bay leaves, a thyme sprig, and a few peppercorns. Partially cover and gently simmer for about 3 hours. Strain the stock into a bowl and cool, then chill. When the stock is completely cold, remove the fat that will have set on the surface.

Stuffings for Chicken

- **Springtime Roast Chicken**
  (see page 87)
- **Chicken with Marmalade Stuffing**
  (see page 89)
- **Pollo Catalan** *(see page 90)*
- **Festive Apple Chicken** *(see page 93)*
- **Traditional Roast Chicken** *(see page 99)*
- **Golden Chicken with Mango & Cranberries** *(see page 100)*

Tips for Reducing Fat without Losing Flavor

- Roast whole chickens with their skin, but remove the skin before serving.
- Use cooking methods that do not require added fat, such as steaming, broiling, stir-frying, baking, and roasting.

Stir-frying: Use just a little oil—once it is hot, it spreads further.

Poaching: Poach chicken in stock with added chopped vegetables. When the chicken is cooked through, purée the vegetables and stock to make a tasty sauce.

Baking: Dip chicken pieces in egg white, then into rolled oats or whole-wheat flour before baking *(see page 61)*.

Steaming: Steam chicken over a smoky flavored tea, such as lapsang souchong.

Grilling: Flavor can be added by first marinating the chicken. On the broiler, fat drips away.

- Make gravy with the meat juices, after skimming off the fat. Add chicken stock and fresh herbs for flavor.
- Remove the skin from chicken pieces and rub a mixture of crushed garlic, chopped fresh herbs, and spices over the chicken before cooking *(see page 78)*.
- Use marinades such as lemon or lime juice, wine, and vinegar to add fat-free flavor.
- Add chopped onion or shallots, either sprinkled over chicken pieces, or placed inside a whole chicken.
- Spread skinless whole chicken or chicken pieces with mustard, or a mixture of honey and mustard with a squeeze of lime juice.
- Serve simply broiled chicken with fruit or vegetable salsas *(see page 65)*.

Soups

Chicken soup has a long tradition of being comforting and good for us and some cultures even think of it as a cure for all ills. It is certainly satisfying, full of flavor and easy to digest. For the best results, choose a boiling fowl or a large roasting bird, because immature birds sold for frying are not flavorful enough to make a tasty soup. Most chicken soups benefit from

being made from a good homemade chicken stock, although when time is at a premium, a good quality bouillon cube can be used instead. Every cuisine in the world has its own favorite version of chicken soup and in this section you will find a selection of recipes from as far afield as Italy, Scotland, and China. The recipes are easy to make and are sure to inspire you to make your own variation of this delicious soup.

Thai Chicken Noodle Soup

Quick to make, this hot and spicy soup is hearty and warming. If you like your food really fiery, add a chopped dried or fresh chili with its seeds.

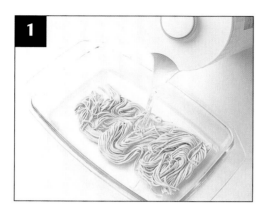

Serves 4–6
1 sheet of dried egg noodles from a 9 ounce pack
1 tbsp oil
4 skinless, boneless chicken thighs, diced
1 bunch scallions, sliced
2 garlic cloves, chopped
³/₄-inch piece fresh ginger root, finely chopped
3³/₄ cups chicken stock
scant 1 cup coconut milk
3 tsp red Thai curry paste
3 tbsp peanut butter
2 tbsp light soy sauce
1 small red bell pepper, chopped
¹/₂ cup frozen peas
salt and pepper

3 Add the drained noodles and heat through. Spoon into bowls and serve with a spoon and fork.

COOK'S VARIATION

Green Thai curry paste can be used instead of red curry paste for a less fiery flavor.

1 Put the noodles in a shallow dish and soak in boiling water, following the pack instructions.

2 Heat the oil in a large saucepan or preheated wok, add the chicken, and stir-fry for 5 minutes, until lightly golden brown all over. Add the white part of the scallions, the garlic, and ginger and stir-fry for 2 minutes. Add the chicken stock, coconut milk, Thai curry paste, peanut butter, and soy sauce. Season to taste with salt and pepper. Bring to a boil, stirring constantly. Lower the heat and simmer, stirring occasionally, for 8 minutes, stirring occasionally. Add the red bell pepper, peas, and green scallion tops and cook for a further 2 minutes.

Chicken Consommé

This is a very flavorful soup, especially if you make it from real chicken stock.
Egg shells are used to give a crystal clear appearance.

Serves 8–10
8 cups chicken stock
$^2/_3$ cup medium sherry
4 egg whites, plus egg shells
4 ounces cooked chicken, thinly sliced
salt and pepper

1 Place the chicken stock and sherry in a large saucepan and heat gently for 5 minutes.

2 Add the egg whites and the egg shells to the chicken stock and whisk until the mixture begins to boil.

3 When the mixture boils, remove the pan from the heat and allow the mixture to subside for 10 minutes. Repeat this process three times.

4 This allows the egg white to trap the sediments in the chicken stock to clarify the soup.

5 Let the consommé cool for about 5 minutes.

6 Carefully place a piece of fine cheesecloth over a clean saucepan. Ladle the soup over the cheesecloth and strain into the saucepan.

7 Repeat this process twice, then gently re-heat the consommé. Season with salt and pepper to taste, add the chicken slices to the consommé, and serve immediately in a warm tureen or individual soup bowls.

Cream of Chicken Soup

Tarragon adds a delicate aniseed flavor to this tasty soup.
If you cannot find tarragon, use parsley for a fresh taste.

Serves 4
4 tbsp sweet butter
1 large onion, chopped
10 ounces cooked chicken, finely shredded
$2^1/_2$ cups chicken stock
1 tbsp chopped fresh tarragon
$^2/_3$ cup heavy cream
salt and pepper
fresh tarragon leaves, to garnish
deep-fried croûtons, to serve

1 Melt the butter in a large saucepan and sauté the onion for 3 minutes.

2 Add the cooked chicken to the pan with $1^1/_4$ cups of the chicken stock.

3 Bring the soup to a boil and simmer for 20 minutes. Allow to cool slightly, then process in a food processor or blender until a smooth purée.

4 Add the remainder of the stock and season to taste with salt and pepper.

5 Add the chopped tarragon, pour the soup into a warm tureen, and add a swirl of cream. Garnish with fresh tarragon and serve immediately with deep-fried croûtons.

COOK'S VARIATION

If you cannot find fresh tarragon, freeze-dried tarragon makes a good substitute. Light cream can be used instead of the heavy cream.

Chicken Wonton Soup

This Chinese-style soup is delicious as a starter
to an Eastern meal or as a light meal.

Serves 4–6
WONTONS
12 ounces ground chicken
1 tbsp soy sauce
1 tsp grated fresh ginger root
1 garlic clove, crushed
2 tsp sherry
2 scallions, chopped
1 tsp sesame oil
1 egg white
$^1\!/_2$ tsp cornstarch
$^1\!/_2$ tsp sugar
about 35 wonton wrappers
SOUP
6 cups chicken stock
1 tbsp light soy sauce
1 scallion, shredded
1 small carrot, very thinly slices

1 Mix together all the ingredients for
the wontons, except the wrappers.

2 Place a small spoonful of the filling
in the center of each wonton wrapper.

3 Dampen the edges and gather up
the wonton wrapper to form a small
pouch enclosing the filling.

4 Cook the filled wontons in boiling
water for 1 minute, or until they float
to the top.

5 Remove with a slotted spoon. Bring
the chicken stock to a boil.

6 Add the soy sauce, scallion, and
carrot. Add the wontons to the soup
and simmer gently for 2 minutes.
Serve at once.

COOK'S TIP

Look for wonton wrappers in
Chinese or Asian supermarkets.
Fresh wrappers can be found in
the chilled compartment and
they can be frozen if you wish.
Wrap in plastic wrap
before freezing.

Dickensian Chicken Broth

This soup is made with traditional Scottish ingredients.
It should be left for at least two days before being re-heated,
then served with oatmeal cakes or bread.

Serves 4
$^1/_3$ cup pre-soaked dried peas
2 pounds diced chicken, fat removed
5 cups chicken stock
$2^1/_2$ cups water
$^1/_4$ cup barley
1 large carrot, diced
1 small turnip, diced
1 large leek, thinly sliced
1 red onion, finely chopped
salt and white pepper

1 Put the peas and chicken into a pan, add the stock and water, and bring slowly to a boil.

2 Skim the stock as it boils.

3 When all the scum has been removed, add the barley and a pinch of salt, and simmer for 35 minutes.

4 Add the rest of the ingredients and simmer for 2 hours.

5 Skim and allow the broth to stand for at least 24 hours. Reheat, adjust the seasoning, and serve.

COOK'S TIP

Use either whole grain barley or pearl barley. Only the outer husk is removed from whole grain barley and when cooked, it has a nutty flavor and a chewy texture.

Tom's Chicken Soup

The potato has been part of the Irish diet for centuries.
This recipe is originally from the north of Ireland, in the
beautiful area of Moira, County Down.

Serves 4
3 slices smoked bacon, chopped
1 pound boneless chicken, chopped
2 tbsp butter
3 medium potatoes, chopped
3 medium onions, chopped
$2\frac{1}{2}$ cups giblet or chicken stock
$2\frac{1}{2}$ cups milk
$\frac{2}{3}$ cup heavy cream
salt and pepper
2 tbsp chopped fresh parsley, to garnish
Irish soda bread, to serve

1 Gently fry the bacon and chicken in a large saucepan for 10 minutes.

2 Add the butter, potatoes, and onions and cook, stirring constantly, for 15 minutes.

3 Add the stock and milk, then bring the soup to a boil, and simmer for 45 minutes. Season with salt and pepper to taste.

4 Blend in the cream and simmer for 5 minutes, garnish with parsley, and serve with Irish soda bread.

COOK'S TIP

Soda bread is not made with yeast as bread usually is. Instead it is made with baking soda as the rising agent. It can be made with all-purpose flour or whole-wheat flour.

Chicken & Pea Soup

A hearty soup that is so simple to make, yet packed with flavor.
You can use either whole green peas or green or yellow split peas.

Serves 4–6

3 slices smoked bacon
finely chopped

2 pounds chicken, chopped

1 large onion, chopped

1 tbsp butter

2¹/₂ cups ready-soaked peas

10 cups chicken stock

²/₃ cup heavy cream

2 tbsp chopped fresh parsley

salt and pepper

cheese croûtes,
to garnish

1 Put the bacon, chicken, and onion into a large saucepan with a little butter and cook over low heat for 8 minutes.

2 Add the peas and stock to the pan, bring to a boil, season lightly with salt and pepper, cover, and simmer for 2 hours.

3 Blend the cream into the soup and transfer to a warm tureen or individual soup bowls. Sprinkle with parsley, top with cheese croûtes, and serve immediately.

COOK'S TIP

Croûtes are slices of French bread that are fried or baked, then they can be sprinkled with grated cheese, and lightly toasted.

Chicken, Guinea Fowl, & Spaghetti Soup

Guinea fowl has a similar texture to chicken, and although it has a milder flavor than other game, it has a slightly gamier flavor than chicken.

Serves 6
1 pound skinless chicken, chopped
1 pound skinless guinea fowl meat, chopped
2$^1/_2$ cups chicken stock
1 small onion
6 peppercorns
1 tsp cloves
pinch of mace
$^2/_3$ cup heavy cream
2 tsp butter
2 tsp all-purpose flour
1 cup quick-cook spaghetti, broken into short lengths and cooked
pepper
2 tbsp chopped fresh parsley, to garnish

1 Put the chicken and guinea fowl meat into a large saucepan, together with the chicken stock.

2 Bring to a boil and add the onion, peppercorns, cloves, and mace. Simmer gently for about 2 hours, until the stock is reduced by about one third.

3 Strain the soup, skim off any fat, and remove any bones from the chicken and the guinea fowl.

4 Transfer the soup and meat to a clean saucepan.

5 Add the heavy cream and bring to a boil over low heat.

6 Melt the butter and stir in the flour to make a paste. Add to the soup and stir until slightly thickened.

7 Just before serving, add the cooked quick-cook spaghetti.

8 Transfer to a warm tureen, garnish with parsley, and serve.

COOK'S VARIATION

Instead of spaghetti, use small pasta shapes, such as ziti or macaroni.

Cream of Chicken & Lemon Soup

A refreshing soup with the fresh flavors of lemon
and parsley is perfect on summer days.

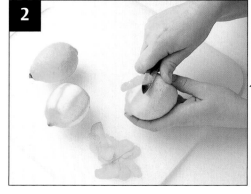

Serves 4
4 tbsp butter
8 shallots, thinly sliced
2 medium carrots, thinly sliced
2 celery stalks, thinly sliced
9 ounces skinless chicken breast meat, finely chopped
3 lemons
5 cups chicken stock
$^2/_3$ cup heavy cream
salt and pepper
sprigs of parsley and lemon slices, to garnish

1 Melt the butter in a large saucepan, add the vegetables and chicken, and cook over low heat for 8 minutes.

2 Thinly pare the lemons and blanch the lemon rind in boiling water for 3 minutes. Drain.

3 Squeeze the juice from the lemons.

4 Add the lemon rind and lemon juice to the pan, together with the chicken stock.

5 Bring to a boil over low heat and simmer for 50 minutes. Cool the soup, then process in a food processor. Return the soup to the saucepan, reheat, season with salt and pepper to taste, and add the heavy cream. Do not allow the soup to boil at this stage or it will curdle.

6 Transfer the soup to a warm tureen or individual bowls. Serve, garnished with parsley and lemon slices.

Cream of Chicken & Tomato Soup

This soup is very good made with fresh tomatoes,
but if you prefer, you can use canned tomatoes.

Serves 2
4 tbsp sweet butter
1 large onion, chopped
1 pound skinless, boneless chicken, very finely shredded
2½ cups chicken stock
6 medium tomatoes, chopped finely
pinch of baking soda
1 tbsp superfine sugar
⅔ cup heavy cream
salt and pepper
fresh basil leaves, to garnish
croûtons, to serve

1 Melt the butter in a large saucepan and fry the onion and shredded chicken for 5 minutes.

2 Add 1¼ cups chicken stock to the pan, together with the tomatoes and baking soda.

3 Bring the soup to a boil and simmer for 20 minutes.

4 Allow the soup to cool, then process in a food processor.

5 Add the remaining chicken stock, season to taste with salt and pepper, then add the sugar.

6 Pour the soup into a warm tureen and add a swirl of cream. Serve immediately with croûtons and garnished with fresh basil leaves.

Cock-a-Leekie Soup

A traditional Scottish soup in which a whole chicken is cooked with vegetables
to add extra flavor to the stock. Add some of the cooked chicken to
the soup and reserve the remainder for another meal.

Serves 4
2–3 pounds oven-ready chicken plus giblets, if available
8–9 cups chicken stock
1 onion, thinly sliced
4 leeks, thinly sliced
pinch of ground allspice or ground coriander seeds
1 bouquet garni, (bay leaf, parsley, and thyme sprigs, tied with string)
12 no-need-to-soak prunes, halved and pitted
salt and pepper
warm crusty bread, to serve

1 Put the chicken and giblets, if
using, stock, and onion in a large
saucepan. Bring to a boil and remove
any scum from the surface.

2 Add the leeks, allspice or coriander,
bouquet garni, and season to taste
with salt and pepper. Cover and
simmer for 1½ hours, until the
chicken is falling off the bone.

3 Remove the chicken from the pan
and skim any fat from the surface of
the soup.

4 Chop some of the chicken flesh and
return it to the pan. Add the prunes,
bring back to a boil, and simmer,
uncovered, for about 20 minutes.

5 Discard the bouquet garni, adjust
the seasoning, and serve.

Chicken Mulligatawny Soup

This spicy soup was brought to the West by army
and service personnel returning from India.

Serves 4
4 tbsp butter
1 onion, sliced
1 garlic clove, crushed
1 pound skinless, boneless chicken, diced
$1/3$ cup diced smoked bacon
1 small turnip, diced
2 carrots, diced
1 small cooking apple, diced
2 tbsp mild curry powder
1 tbsp curry paste
1 tbsp tomato paste
1 tbsp all-purpose flour
5 cups chicken stock
$2/3$ cup heavy cream
salt and pepper
1 tsp of chopped fresh cilantro, to garnish
boiled or fried rice, to serve

1 Melt the butter in a large saucepan
and cook the onion, garlic, chicken,
and bacon for 5 minutes.

2 Add the turnip, carrots, and apple
and cook for a further 2 minutes.

3 Blend in the curry powder, curry
paste, and tomato paste, and sprinkle
in the flour.

4 Add the chicken stock and bring to
a boil, cover, and simmer for 1 hour.

5 Process the soup in a food
processor. Reheat, season to taste, and
gradually blend in the cream. Garnish
with coriander and serve over small
bowls of boiled or fried rice.

Cream of Chicken & Orange Soup

For a tangy flavor, lemons can be used instead of oranges and the recipe
can be adapted to make duck and orange soup.

Serves 4
4 tbsp butter
8 shallots, thinly sliced
2 medium carrots, thinly sliced
2 celery stalks, thinly sliced
8 ounces skinless chicken breast finely chopped
3 oranges
5 cups chicken stock
$2/3$ cup heavy cream
salt and white pepper
sprig of parsley and 3 orange slices, to garnish
soda bread, to serve

1 Melt the butter in a large saucepan,
add the vegetables and chicken meat,
and cook gently for 8 minutes.

2 Thinly pare the oranges and blanch
the rind in boiling water for about
3 minutes. Drain.

3 Squeeze the juice from the oranges.
Add the orange rind and orange juice
to the pan with the chicken stock.

4 Bring to a boil over low heat and
simmer for 50 minutes. Cool the soup
then process in a blender or food
processor until smooth.

COOK'S VARIATION

Use 2 small lemons in place of
the oranges. Look for organic or
unwaxed lemons when using rind.

5 Return the soup to the pan, re-heat,
season to taste with salt and pepper,
and add the cream. Do not allow the
soup to boil or it will curdle.

6 Transfer the soup to a warm tureen
or individual bowls, and serve,
garnished with a sprig of parsley,
orange slices, and soda bread.

Chicken Soup with Cilantro Dumplings

Use the strained vegetables and chicken to make little patties. Simply mash with a little butter, shape them into round cakes, and fry in butter or oil until golden brown.

Serves 6–8

2 pounds chicken
meat, sliced

$^1/_2$ cup all-purpose flour

$^1/_2$ cup butter

3 tbsp sunflower oil

1 large carrot, chopped

1 celery stalk, chopped

1 onion, chopped

1 small turnip, chopped

$^1/_2$ cup sherry

1 tsp thyme

1 bay leaf

8 cups chicken stock

salt and pepper

crusty bread,
to serve

DUMPLINGS

$^1/_2$ cup self-rising flour

1 cup fresh bread crumbs

2 tbsp shredded suet

2 tbsp chopped fresh cilantro

2 tbsp finely grated lemon rind

1 egg

salt and pepper

1 Coat the chicken pieces lightly with the flour and season with salt and pepper.

2 Melt the butter in a saucepan and fry the chicken pieces until they are lightly browned all over.

3 Add the sunflower oil to the pan and brown all of the vegetables together. Add the sherry with all the remaining ingredients, except the chicken stock.

4 Cook, stirring frequently, for 10 minutes, then gradually add the chicken stock. Simmer for 3 hours, skimming off any excess fat from time to time.

5 Strain the liquid into a large clean saucepan and set aside to cool.

6 To make the dumplings, mix together the flour, bread crumbs, suet, cilantro, and lemon rind in a large mixing bowl.

7 Blend in the egg, then add enough milk to make a moist dough.

8 Shape the dough into small balls and roll them in a little flour.

9 Cook the dumplings in boiling lightly salted water for 10 minutes.

10 Transfer the dumplings to the soup with a slotted spoon. Cook for a further 12 minutes, then serve the soup with crusty bread.

Chicken & Leek Soup

This satisfying soup can be served as a main course.
You can add rice and bell peppers to make it even heartier, as well as colorful.

Serves 6
2 tbsp butter
12 ounces boneless chicken, diced
12 ounces leeks, cut into 1-inch pieces
5 cups chicken stock
1 bouquet garni sachet
salt and white pepper
8 pitted prunes, halved
cooked rice and diced bell peppers (optional)

1 Melt the butter in a large saucepan, add the chicken and leeks, and fry for 8 minutes.

2 Add the chicken stock and bouquet garni sachet, and season with salt and pepper to taste.

3 Bring the soup to a boil and simmer for 45 minutes.

4 Add the prunes with some cooked rice and diced bell peppers, if you desired, and simmer for 20 minutes. Remove and discard the bouquet garni sachet. Transfer the soup to a warm tureen or individual bowls and serve immediately.

COOK'S TIP

Instead of the bouquet garni sachet, you can use a bunch of fresh, mixed herbs, tied together with string. Choose herbs such as parsley, thyme, and rosemary.

Chicken & Corn Soup

A hint of chili and sherry flavor this chicken and corn soup,
which has both baby corn cobs and corn kernels in it,
with red bell pepper and tomato for color and flavor.

Serves 4
1 skinless, boneless chicken breast, about 6 ounces
2 tbsp sunflower oil
2–3 scallions, thinly sliced diagonally
1 small or ½ large red bell pepper, thinly sliced
1 garlic clove, crushed
4 ounces baby corn cobs, thinly sliced
4 cups chicken stock
7 ounce can corn well drained
2 tbsp sherry
2–3 tsp sweet chili sauce
2–3 tsp cornstarch
2 tomatoes, quartered, seeded, and sliced
salt and pepper
chopped fresh cilantro or parsley, to garnish

1 With a sharp knife, cut the chicken breast into 4 strips lengthwise, then cut each strip into narrow slices across the grain.

2 Heat the oil in a preheated wok or skillet, swirling it around until it is really hot and coating the sides of the pan. Add the chicken and stir-fry for 3–4 minutes, moving it around the wok until it is well sealed all over and almost cooked through.

3 Add the scallions, bell pepper, and garlic, and stir-fry for 2–3 minutes. Add the baby corn and chicken stock and bring to a boil.

4 Add the corn kernels, sherry, sweet chili sauce, and salt to taste, and simmer for 5 minutes, stirring from time to time.

5 Blend the cornstarch with a little cold water. Add to the soup and bring to a boil, stirring until the sauce is thickened. Add the tomato slices, season with salt and pepper to taste, and simmer for 1–2 minutes. Serve the soup hot, sprinkled with chopped cilantro or parsley.

Chicken Soup with Almonds

This soup can also be made using turkey or pheasant breasts.
Pheasant gives a stronger flavor, particularly if game stock
is made from the carcass and used in the soup.

Serves 4
1 large or 2 small skinless, boneless chicken breasts
1 tbsp sunflower oil
1 carrot, cut into julienne strips
4 scallions, thinly sliced diagonally
3 cups chicken stock
finely grated rind of $\frac{1}{2}$ lemon
$\frac{1}{3}$ cup ground almonds
1 tbsp light soy sauce
1 tbsp lemon juice
$\frac{1}{2}$ cup slivered almonds, toasted
salt and pepper
bread, to serve

5 Adjust the seasoning, add most of the toasted slivered almonds, and cook for a further 1–2 minutes.

6 Serve the soup very hot, in individual bowls, sprinkled with the remaining almonds.

COOK'S VARIATION

If you prefer, use finely chopped, skinless toasted hazelnuts in place of the slivered almonds.

1 Using a sharp knife, cut each chicken breast into four strips lengthwise, then slice very thinly across the grain into shreds.

2 Heat the oil in a preheated wok or skillet, swirling it around until really hot. Add the chicken and stir-fry for 3–4 minutes, until sealed and almost cooked through. Add the carrot and stir-fry for 2–3 minutes. Add the scallions and stir.

3 Add the stock to the wok and bring to a boil. Add the lemon rind, ground almonds, soy sauce, lemon juice, and plenty of salt and pepper.

4 Bring back to a boil and simmer, uncovered, for 5 minutes, stirring.

Vegetable & Garbanzo Bean Soup

A good tasty soup full of vegetables, chicken, and garbanzo beans,
with just a hint of spiciness, to serve on any occasion.

Serves 4–6
3 tbsp olive oil
1 large onion, finely chopped
2–3 garlic cloves, crushed
$^1/_2$–1 red chili, seeded and very finely chopped
1 skinless, boneless chicken breast, about 5 ounces, thickly sliced
2 celery stalks, finely chopped
6 ounces carrots, coarsely grated
$5^2/_3$ cups chicken stock
2 bay leaves
$^1/_2$ tsp dried oregano
$^1/_4$ tsp ground cinnamon
14 ounce can garbanzo beans, drained
2 medium tomatoes, peeled, seeded, and chopped
1 tbsp tomato paste
salt and pepper
chopped fresh cilantro or parsley, to garnish
warm corn or wheat tortillas, to serve

1 Heat the oil in a large saucepan and sauté the onion, garlic, and chili until they are softened but not colored.

2 Add the chicken to the saucepan and continue to cook until well sealed and lightly browned.

3 Add the celery, carrots, stock, bay leaves, oregano, and cinnamon and season to taste with salt and pepper. Bring to a boil, then cover, and simmer gently for about 20 minutes, or until the chicken is tender and cooked through.

4 Remove the chicken from the soup and chop it finely, or cut it into narrow strips.

5 Return the chicken to the pan with the garbanzo beans, tomatoes, and tomato paste. Simmer, covered, for a

further 15–20 minutes. Discard the bay leaves, then adjust the seasoning.

6 Serve very hot, sprinkled with cilantro or parsley and accompanied by warm tortillas.

Chicken & Pasta Broth

This satisfying soup makes a good lunch or supper dish and you can use any vegetables that you have at hand. Children will love the tiny pasta shapes.

Serves 6
12 ounces boneless chicken breasts
2 tbsp sunflower oil
1 medium onion, diced
1^1/$_2$ cups diced carrots
8 ounces cauliflower flowerets
3 ^{3}/$_4$ cups chicken stock
2 tsp dried mixed herbs
1 cup small pasta shapes
salt and pepper
Parmesan cheese (optional) and crusty bread, to serve

1 Finely dice the chicken, discarding any skin.

2 Heat the oil in a large pan and quickly sauté the chicken and vegetables until they are lightly colored.

3 Stir in the stock and herbs. Bring to a boil and add the pasta. Return to a boil, cover, and simmer for about 10 minutes. Season to taste with salt and pepper. Transfer to a warm tureen or individual soup bowls and sprinkle with Parmesan cheese, if using. Serve with crusty bread.

COOK'S VARIATION

Broccoli flowerets can be used to replace the cauliflower flowerets. Substitute 2 tablespoons chopped fresh mixed herbs for the dried mixed herbs.

Chicken & Chestnut Soup

A rich soup based on a good stock with pieces of chicken and chopped chestnuts for an interesting flavor and texture.

Serves 4–6
2 onions
raw or cooked chicken carcass, chopped, plus trimmings
chicken giblets, if available
6¼ cups water
1 bouquet garni, (bay leaf, parsley, and thyme sprigs, tied with string)
½ cup fresh chestnuts, pierced and roasted for about 5 minutes or boiled for 30–40 minutes, and drained, or 1 cup canned peeled chestnuts
3 tbsp butter or margarine
⅓ cup all-purpose flour
⅔ cup milk
½ tsp ground coriander seeds
1½ cups coarsely grated carrots
1 tbsp chopped fresh parsley (optional)
salt and pepper

1 Cut one of the onions into quarters. Put the chicken carcass, giblets, if available, water, the quartered onion, and bouquet garni into a saucepan. Bring to a boil, cover, and simmer stirring occasionally, for about 1 hour.

2 Strain and measure the stock. Reserve 4 cups.

3 Remove ½–¾ cup of chicken trimmings from the carcass and chop finely. If using canned chestnuts, drain well; if using fresh chestnuts, peel them. Finely chop the chestnuts. Chop the remaining onion.

4 Melt the butter or margarine in a saucepan and sauté the onion gently until soft. Stir in the flour and cook over a low heat for 1–2 minutes.

5 Gradually stir in the reserved stock and bring to a boil over low heat. Simmer, stirring constantly, for 2 minutes, then add the milk, ground coriander, chopped chicken, carrots, and chestnuts. Season to taste with salt and pepper.

6 Bring the soup back to a boil and simmer for 10 minutes, then stir in the parsley, if using. Adjust the seasoning before serving.

Chicken & Corn Chowder

A quick and satisfying soup, full of flavor and different textures.
Corn cobs are a sweet, juicy addition.

Serves 2
2 tsp oil
$^{1}/_{4}$ cup butter or margarine
1 small onion, finely chopped
1 chicken leg, quarter, or 2–3 drumsticks
1 tbsp all-purpose flour
$2^{1}/_{2}$ cups chicken stock
$^{1}/_{2}$ small red, yellow, or orange bell pepper, finely chopped
2 large tomatoes, peeled and chopped
2 tsp tomato paste
7 ounce can corn, drained
pinch of dried oregano
$^{1}/_{4}$ tsp ground coriander seeds
salt and pepper
chopped fresh parsley, to garnish
crusty bread, to serve

1 Heat the oil and butter or margarine in a saucepan and sauté the onion gently until just beginning to soften. Cut the chicken quarter, if using, into 2 pieces. Add the chicken to the saucepan and fry, turning frequently, until golden brown all over.

2 Add the flour and cook, stirring constantly, for 1–2 minutes. Then gradually add the stock, bring to a boil, and simmer for about 5 minutes.

3 Add the bell pepper, tomatoes, tomato paste, corn, oregano, and coriander. Season to taste with salt

and pepper. Cover and simmer gently for about 20 minutes, until the chicken is very tender.

4 Remove the chicken from the soup, strip the flesh from the bone, and chop it finely with a sharp knife. Then return the chicken to the soup.

5 Adjust the seasoning and simmer for a further 2–3 minutes before sprinkling with chopped, fresh parsley. Serve the soup very hot with crusty bread.

Noodles in Soup

Noodles in soup are popular in China. This is a thick, hearty soup, just add more stock if you prefer a thinner soup.

Serves 4
8 ounces cooked, skinless, boneless chicken
3–4 Chinese dried mushrooms, soaked in hot water
4 ounce can of sliced bamboo shoots, rinsed and drained
4 ounces spinach, lettuce hearts, or Chinese cabbage
2 scallions
8 ounces egg noodles
about 2½ cups chicken stock
2 tbsp light soy sauce
2 tbsp vegetable oil
1 tsp salt
½ tsp sugar
2 tsp Chinese rice wine or dry sherry
a few drops of sesame oil
1 tsp red chili oil (optional)

1 With a sharp knife, cut the chicken into thin shreds. Squeeze dry the soaked mushrooms and discard the hard stalks.

2 Thinly shred the Chinese mushrooms, bamboo shoots, spinach, lettuce hearts, or Chinese cabbage, and scallions.

3 Cook the noodles in boiling water according to the instructions on the packet, then drain, and rinse under cold water. Place the noodles in a tureen or serving bowl and set aside. Bring the stock to a boil, add about 1 tablespoon soy sauce, and pour the mixture over the noodles. Keep warm.

4 Heat the oil in a preheated wok or heavy-based skillet and add about half the scallions, the chicken, Chinese mushrooms, bamboo shoots, and spinach, lettuce hearts, or Chinese cabbage. Stir-fry for about 2–3 minutes. Add the remaining soy sauce, salt, sugar, Chinese rice wine or

sherry, sesame oil and, chili oil, if using, and blend together well.

5 Pour the mixture in the wok over the noodles, garnish with the remaining scallions, and serve the soup immediately.

Hot & Sour Soup

This is one of the most popular soups in Chinese
restaurants throughout the world.

Serves 4

4–6 dried shiitake mushrooms,
soaked in hot water

4 ounces cooked chicken

1 cake bean curd

2 ounce can sliced
bamboo shoots, drained

1 tbsp cornstarch

$2\frac{1}{2}$ cups chicken stock or water

1 tbsp Chinese rice wine
or dry sherry

1 tbsp light soy sauce

2 tbsp rice vinegar

$\frac{1}{2}$ tsp ground white pepper

salt

2–3 scallions, thinly sliced,
to garnish

1 Drain the mushrooms, squeeze
dry, and discard the hard stalks.
Thinly slice the caps.

2 Thinly slice the chicken, bean curd,
and bamboo shoots into narrow
shreds using a cleaver.

3 Mix the cornstarch with
$1\frac{1}{2}$ tablespoons water to form a
smooth paste and set aside.

4 Bring the stock or water to a rolling
boil in a wok or skillet and add the
mushrooms, chicken, tofu, and
bamboo shoots. Bring back to a boil,
then simmer for about 1 minute.

5 Add the Chinese rice wine or
sherry, soy sauce and rice vinegar.
Bring back to a boil and stir in the
cornstarch paste. Add the pepper and

season with salt to taste. Transfer to a
warm tureen or individual soup bowls
and serve hot, sprinkled with the
sliced scallions.

COOK'S TIP

Shiitake mushrooms have a
pronounced flavor. Wipe the caps
and stalks before cooking.

Chicken & Noodle One-Pot

Flavorful chicken and vegetables cooked with Chinese egg noodles in a coconut sauce.
Increase the amount of stock for a thinner soup. Serve the soup in deep bowls.

Serves 4
1 tbsp sunflower oil
1 onion, sliced
1 garlic clove, crushed
1-inch piece fresh ginger root, grated
1 bunch scallions, sliced diagonally
1 pound skinless, boneless chicken breasts, cut into bite-size pieces
2 tbsp mild curry paste
2 cups coconut milk
1¼ cups chicken stock
8 ounces Chinese egg noodles
2 tsp lime juice
salt and pepper
sprigs of basil, to garnish

5 Add the lime juice and season to taste with salt and pepper. Transfer to individual deep soup bowls, garnish with basil sprigs, and serve at once.

COOK'S TIP

Look for canned coconut milk in Asian and Chinese supermarkets or in delicatessens.

1 Heat the oil in a preheated wok or large, heavy-based skillet. Add the onion, garlic, ginger, and scallions and stir-fry for 2 minutes, until softened.

2 Add the chicken pieces and curry paste. Stir-fry for about 4 minutes, until the vegetables and chicken are golden brown.

3 Stir in the coconut milk and stock and season with salt and pepper to taste, mixing until well blended. Bring to a boil.

4 Add the noodles to the wok or skillet. Cover and simmer stirring occasionally, for about 6–8 minutes, until the noodles are just tender, but still firm to the bite.

Starters, Snacks, & Salads

Chicken is versatile and quick to cook, making it perfect for innovative and appetizing first courses or light lunches. Its unassertive flavor means that it can be enlivened by exotic fruits and spices and Eastern ingredients, such as mirin, sesame oil, and fresh ginger root. It is infused with a spicy Middle Eastern flavor after marinating in a rich mixture of spices, then

served in pita bread with salad and herbed yogurt. There are fritters, classic salads, rarebits, pâtés, potted chicken, sandwiches, fillings for baked potatoes, and drumsticks that are stuffed and baked, or served with delicious fruity salsas. Because chicken pieces travel well and are easy to eat, many of the recipes are ideal to take on picnics or to pack for lunch. The recipes are cosmopolitan, with influences appearing from as far apart as the Mediterranean and Asia.

Oriental Chicken Salad

Mirin, soy sauce, and sesame oil give an Eastern
flavor to this fresh-tasting salad.

Serves 4
1¹/₂ pounds skinless boneless chicken
¹/₃ cup mirin or sweet sherry
¹/₃ cup light soy sauce
1 tbsp sesame oil
3 tbsp olive oil
1 tbsp red wine vinegar
1 tbsp Dijon mustard
8 ounces egg noodles
4 cups bean sprouts
4 cups shredded Chinese cabbage
2 scallions, sliced
1³/₄ cups sliced mushrooms

1 Place the chicken pieces between
two sheets of plastic wrap and pound
with a rolling pin, cleaver, or meat
mallet until they are flattened to an
even thickness.

2 Put the chicken in a roasting pan.
Combine the mirin and soy sauce and
brush the mixture over the chicken.
Cook in a preheated oven at 400°F for
20–30 minutes, basting frequently
with the mirin and soy sauce mixture.
Remove from the oven and set aside
to cool slightly.

3 Meanwhile, combine the sesame
oil, olive oil, and vinegar with the
Dijon mustard in a serving bowl.

4 Cook the noodles according to the
packet instructions. Rinse under cold
running water, then drain, and
immediately toss in the sesame and
mustard dressing.

5 Add the bean sprouts, Chinese
cabbage, scallions, and mushrooms to
and toss to coat with the dressing.

6 Slice the cooked chicken very thinly
and stir into the noodles. Serve the
salad immediately.

Chicken, Papaya, & Avocado Salad

Try this recipe with peaches or nectarines instead of papaya.

Serves 4
4 skinless, boneless chicken breasts
1 red chili seeded and chopped
$1^1/_2$ tbsp red wine vinegar
$^1/_3$ cup olive oil
1 papaya, peeled
1 avocado, peeled, halved, and pitted
4 ounces alfalfa sprouts
4 ounces bean sprouts
salt and pepper

1 Poach the chicken breasts in boiling water for 15 minutes, or until cooked through. Remove with a slotted spoon and set aside to cool.

2 Combine the chili, vinegar, and oil, season well with salt and pepper, and set aside.

3 Thinly slice the chicken breasts with a sharp knife.

4 Slice the papaya and avocado to the same thickness as the chicken. Arrange on four plates with the alfalfa sprouts and bean sprouts. Serve accompanied by the dressing.

COOK'S TIP

If you are using papaya rather than peaches in this recipe, add a little lime juice and grated lime rind to the chili dressing, for an extra tangy flavor.

Veronica Salad

A delicious salad consisting of strips of cooked chicken with grapes,
celery, and hard-cooked eggs in a lightly curried,
minty dressing garnished with Belgian endive.

Serves 6
4 skinless, boneless chicken breasts
2 tbsp olive oil
1 tbsp sunflower oil
1–2 garlic cloves, crushed
1 onion, finely chopped
2 tbsp chopped fresh mint
4 green celery stalks
1¹/₂ cups black grapes, preferably seedless
1 cup large green seedless grapes
2 tbsp butter or margarine
1 tbsp all-purpose flour
¹/₂ tsp curry powder
3 tbsp white wine or stock
5 tbsp milk
2 tbsp ricotta cheese
2 tbsp mayonnaise
1 Belgian endive
2 hard-cooked eggs, quartered
salt and pepper

1 Cut the chicken into strips. Heat the oils in a skillet, add the garlic and chicken, and fry gently until well sealed. Add the onion and fry until the chicken and onion are tender.

2 Stir in the mint and plenty of salt and pepper. Immediately drain off the oil and juices. Put the chicken mixture into a bowl and set aside until cold.

3 Cut the celery into thin diagonal slices and add to the chicken.

4 Reserve a few whole black grapes for garnish. If they are large or contain pips, cut the remainder in half, remove any pips and then add to the salad with the green grapes.

5 Melt the butter or margarine in a pan, stir in the flour and curry powder, and cook for 1–2 minutes. Add the wine or stock and the milk, and bring to a boil, then simmer until thick. Remove from the heat, season with salt and pepper to taste, and stir in the ricotta. Cover with plastic wrap and set aside until cold.

6 Stir the mayonnaise into the sauce and add to the chicken mixture. Turn into a serving dish. Arrange the Belgian endive around the edge of the salad with the reserved grapes and hard-cooked egg quarters. Cover and chill until ready to serve.

Chicken Pasta Provençale

Use any pasta shapes for this salad, but drain thoroughly
so that it does not dilute the dressing.

Serves 4
1¹/₂ cups dried pasta shapes
4 tbsp French Dressing (see below)
2 tbsp olive oil
12 ounces skinless, boneless chicken breast, cut into strips
2 zucchini, sliced
1 red bell pepper, seeded and cut into chunks
2 garlic cloves, sliced
4 tomatoes, cut into wedges
2 ounce can anchovies, drained and chopped
¹/₄ cup pitted black olives, halved
sprig of fresh parsley, to garnish

FRENCH DRESSING

3 tbsp olive oil
1 tbsp wine vinegar
1 garlic clove, crushed
¹/₂ tsp Dijon or Meaux mustard
1 tsp clear honey
salt and pepper

1 Cook the pasta in boiling lightly salted water for 10–12 minutes, until tender, but still firm to the bite. Drain thoroughly.

2 Whisk all the dressing ingredients together until thoroughly blended.

3 Put the pasta into a bowl with the dressing and mix together.

4 Heat the oil in a skillet. Add the chicken and stir-fry for 4–5 minutes, until cooked. Remove from the pan.

5 Add the zucchini, bell pepper, and garlic to the skillet. Fry, stirring frequently, for about 12–15 minutes, until softened.

6 Add the tomatoes, anchovies, and olives to the pasta with the chicken and fried vegetables, and mix thoroughly together.

7 Transfer to a serving dish, garnish with parsley, and serve immediately while warm.

Chicken Liver & Watercress Pâté

The peppery flavors of the watercress really come through in this soft pâté—try serving it on hot Melba toast as a delicious snack.

Serves 4–6
1/4 cup butter
1 onion, chopped
8 ounces chicken livers
1 garlic clove, chopped
4 ounces watercress, trimmed and chopped
1 tbsp chopped fresh thyme
1 tbsp chopped fresh parsley
1 tbsp sherry
salt and pepper
sprig of watercress, to garnish
hot Melba toast, to serve

1 Heat the butter in a skillet and sauté the onion gently for about 5 minutes, until soft.

2 Add the chicken livers and garlic and sauté gently for 3–4 minutes, until cooked through.

3 Set aside to cool slightly, before stirring in the watercress, fresh herbs, and sherry.

4 Transfer the mixture to a food processor and process until the chicken livers are finely chopped, but still have some texture. Alternatively, put the mixture through a food mill.

5 Transfer the mixture to a serving dish. Cover and chill in the refrigerator. Serve, garnished with watercress, with hot Melba toast.

Potted Chicken

Cooked poultry, meat, and game can all be prepared in this traditional way:
finely ground and cooked with onions, spices, and sherry or port.
Serve as a first course or use as a sandwich filling.

Serves 4–6

8 ounces boneless
cooked chicken leg meat

¹/₂ cup butter

1 onion, very finely chopped

1–2 garlic cloves, crushed

2 tbsp sherry or port

about 4 tbsp stock

pinch of ground mace,
nutmeg, or allspice

pinch of dried mixed herbs

salt and pepper

sprigs of fresh thyme, to garnish

TO SERVE

sprigs of watercress

cherry tomatoes
or tomato wedges

crusty bread or fingers of toast

1 Remove any skin and gristle from the meat. Finely grind twice in a meat grinder, or process in a food processor until finely chopped.

2 Melt half the butter in a saucepan and sauté the onion and garlic gently until soft, but only lightly colored.

3 Stir the chicken into the pan, followed by the sherry or port and just enough of the stock to moisten the mixture.

4 Season to taste with salt, pepper, mace, nutmeg or allspice, and herbs. Press the mixture into a lightly greased dish or several small individual dishes and level the top. Cover and chill until firm.

5 Melt the remaining butter and pour a thin layer over the potted chicken. Gently press in a few sprigs of thyme and chill thoroughly so that the herbs set in the butter.

6 Serve spooned onto plates, or in individual pots on plates, garnished with watercress, with tomatoes and crusty bread or fingers of toast.

Chicken in Pita Bread

Pita bread makes a great container for fast and flavorful meals—either on the move or for a weekend lunch.

Serves 4
1 tbsp cumin seeds, crushed
1 tbsp coriander seeds, crushed
1 tbsp ground turmeric
1 tbsp black mustard seeds
2 tsp chili flakes
$1/4$ cup olive oil
$1^{1}/_{2}$ pounds skinless, boneless chicken thighs
$1^{1}/_{4}$ cups unsweetened yogurt
3 cups fresh cilantro
3 cups fresh mint
juice of 1 lime
salt and pepper
sprigs of fresh parsley, to garnish
TO SERVE
4 pita breads
salad greens
cucumber slices
tomato wedges
baby tomatoes

1 Combine the cumin, coriander, turmeric, mustard seeds, chili flakes, and oil. Season generously with salt and pepper.

2 Cut the chicken into finger width strips and place in a large bowl. Toss in the spice mixture. Set aside to marinate for at least 2 hours, or as long as possible.

3 Cook the chicken in a preheated oven at 425°F for 15 minutes, turning once or twice.

4 Put the yogurt and herbs in a food processor and process until smooth,

or finely chop the fresh herbs and stir into the yogurt. Add the lime juice and season well with salt and pepper.

5 To serve, split the pita breads and warm them through. Stuff generously

with salad greens, cucumber, and tomatoes, and divide the chicken strips among them. Spoon over a little yogurt dressing and serve, garnished with parsley sprigs.

Super Club Sandwich

Club sandwiches are intended to be more or less adequate substitutes for
a full meal and can be as many layers high as you can manage!

Serves 1
3 slices white or brown bread
¼ cup butter
4 ounces cooked skinless, boneless chicken, shredded
3 tbsp lemon mayonnaise
4 small crisp lettuce leaves
1 tomato, sliced
2-inch piece cucumber, sliced
salt and pepper

TO GARNISH

sprigs of watercress
lemon wedges

1 Toast the slices of bread on both sides until golden, then spread each slice with butter.

2 In a small bowl, mix the chicken with the mayonnaise and season with salt and pepper to taste.

3 Cover the first slice of toast with two of the lettuce leaves, then half of the chicken mixture, and all of the tomato slices.

4 Cover with the second slice of toast, then the remaining chicken mixture, and the sliced cucumber.

5 Place the third slice of toast on top, buttered side down, and press gently to seal.

6 With a sharp knife, cut the whole sandwich into two large triangles or alternatively into quarters, and secure each with a toothpick, if desired. Serve garnished with sprigs of watercress and lemon wedges.

COOK'S VARIATION

Shredded iceberg lettuce, instead of leaves, adds a crunchy texture.

Spiced Chicken Koftas

Koftas are spicy balls of ground poultry or meat. In this recipe
they are made with chicken, but you could use lamb or beef. Lime pickle
is available in Asian foodstores and some supermarkets.

Serves 4
1 pound skinless, boneless chicken, coarsley chopped
1 garlic clove
1-inch piece fresh ginger root, grated
$^1/_2$ green bell pepper, seeded and coarsely chopped
2 fresh green chilies, seeded and chopped
4 tsp garam masala
$^1/_2$ tsp ground turmeric
2 tbsp chopped fresh cilantro
$^1/_2$ tsp salt
6 tbsp vegetable oil
lime pickle and lime wedges, to serve

1 Put all the ingredients, except the oil and lime pickle, into a food processor or blender and process until the mixture is finely chopped. Alternatively, chop the chicken, garlic, ginger, bell pepper, and chilies very finely, and mix together in a bowl with the garam masala, turmeric, cilantro, and salt.

2 Shape the mixture between the palms of your hands to form 16 small evenly-shaped balls.

3 Heat the oil in a preheated wok or large skillet and fry the koftas, turning occasionally, for about 8–10 minutes until browned all over and cooked through. If you cannot fit all the koftas into the wok or skillet at once, cook them in batches. Keep the first batch warm in a low oven while you fry the rest.

4 Drain on paper towels and serve with lime pickle and lime wedges.

Thai Chicken Spring Rolls

A cucumber dipping sauce tastes perfect with these delicious spring rolls,
filled with chicken and fresh, crunchy vegetables.

Serves 4
1 tbsp light soy sauce
1 tsp sugar
2 tsp cornstarch, blended with 2 tbsp cold water
2 tbsp vegetable oil
4 scallions, trimmed and very finely sliced
1 carrot, cut into matchstick strips
1 small green or red bell pepper, seeded and finely sliced
$2/3$ cup sliced button mushrooms
1 cup bean sprouts
1 cup cooked skinless, boneless chicken, shredded
8-inch spring roll wrappers
oil for deep-frying
salt and pepper
scallion brushes, to garnish

DIPPING SAUCE

$1/4$ cup light malt vinegar
2 tbsp water
$1/4$ cup light brown sugar
$1/2$ tsp salt
2-inch piece of cucumber, peeled and finely chopped
4 scallions, trimmed and finely sliced
1 small red or green chili, seeded and very finely chopped

1 Mix together the soy sauce, sugar, and cornstarch paste.

2 Heat the oil in a preheated wok or skillet and add the scallions, carrot, and bell pepper. Stir-fry for 2–3 minutes. Add the mushrooms, bean sprouts, and chicken and cook for a further 2 minutes. Season to taste with salt and pepper.

3 Add the cornstarch mixture to the wok or skillet and cook, stirring constantly, for about 1 minute, until thickened. Set aside to cool.

4 Place spoonfuls of the chicken mixture onto the spring roll wrappers. Dampen the edges and roll them up to enclose the filling.

5 To make the dipping sauce, heat the vinegar, water, sugar, and salt in a saucepan. Boil for 1 minute. Mix the cucumber, scallions, and chili in a small serving bowl and pour in the vinegar mixture. Cool.

6 Heat the oil for deep-frying and fry the rolls until crisp and golden brown. Drain well on paper towels, then serve, garnished with scallion brushes and accompanied by the cucumber dipping sauce.

Chicken Scallops

Served in scallop shells, this dish makes a stylish
presentation for a dinner-party first course.

Serves 4
1²/₃ cups short-cut macaroni, or other short dried pasta shapes
3 tbsp vegetable oil, plus extra for brushing
1 onion, finely chopped
3 slices unsmoked bacon, chopped
1¹/₂ cups button mushrooms, thinly sliced
³/₄ cup cooked skinless, boneless chicken, diced
³/₄ cup crème fraîche or sour cream
4 tbsp dry bread crumbs
¹/₂ cup grated sharp Cheddar cheese
salt and pepper
sprigs of flat leaf parsley, to garnish

1 Cook the pasta in a large pan of boiling lightly salted water to which you have added 1 tablespoon of the oil. When the pasta is tender, but still firm to the bite, drain through a colander, return to the pan, cover, and keep warm.

2 Heat the remaining oil in a pan over medium heat and sauté the onion for 3–4 minutes, until it is translucent. Add the chopped bacon and mushrooms and cook, stirring once or twice, for a further 3–4 minutes.

3 Stir in the drained pasta, diced chicken, and the crème fraîche or sour cream, and season with salt and pepper to taste.

4 Brush four large scallop shells with oil. Spoon in the chicken mixture and smooth to make neat mounds.

5 Mix together the bread crumbs and grated cheese, and sprinkle over the

top of the shells. Press the topping lightly into the chicken mixture, and place under a preheated broiler for 4–5 minutes, until golden brown and bubbling. Garnish with parsley sprigs, and serve hot.

Chicken Pepperonata

All the sunshine colors and flavors of the Mediterranean
are combined in this easy dish.

Serves 4
8 skinless chicken thighs
2 tbsp whole-wheat flour
2 tbsp olive oil
1 small onion, thinly sliced
1 garlic clove, crushed
1 each large red, yellow, and green bell peppers, seeded and thinly sliced
14 ounce can chopped tomatoes
1 tbsp chopped oregano
salt and pepper
fresh oregano, to garnish
crusty whole-wheat bread, to serve

1 Remove the skin from the chicken thighs and toss in the flour.

2 Heat the oil in a wide pan and fry the chicken quickly until sealed and lightly browned, then remove from the pan. Add the onion to the pan and gently sauté until soft. Add the garlic, bell peppers, tomatoes, and oregano, bring to a boil, stirring.

3 Arrange the chicken on top of the vegetables, season well with salt and pepper, then cover the pan tightly,

and simmer for 20–25 minutes, or until the chicken is completely cooked through and tender.

4 Season to taste, garnish with oregano, and serve with crusty whole-wheat bread.

COOK'S TIP

For extra flavor, halve the bell peppers and broil under a preheated broiler until the skins are charred. Let cool, then remove the skins and seeds. Slice the bell peppers thinly and use in the recipe.

Chicken Pan Bagna

Perfect for a picnic or packed lunch, this Mediterranean-style
sandwich can be prepared ahead.

Serves 6
1 long French loaf
1 garlic clove
$\frac{1}{2}$ cup olive oil
$2\frac{3}{4}$ ounce can anchovy fillets
12 ounces cold roast chicken
2 large tomatoes, sliced
8 large, pitted black olives, chopped
pepper

1 Cut the French loaf in half
lengthwise and open out.

2 Cut the garlic clove in half and rub
it, cut side down, over the cut
surfaces of the bread. Sprinkle the cut
surface of the bread with the oil.

3 Drain the anchovies, thinly slice
the chicken, and arrange them over
the bread with the tomatoes.

4 Scatter with black olives and plenty
of pepper. Sandwich the loaf back
together and wrap tightly in foil until
required. Cut into slices to serve.

COOK'S TIP

Arrange a few fresh basil leaves in
between the tomato slices to add a
warm, spicy flavor. Use a good
quality olive oil in this recipe for
extra flavor.

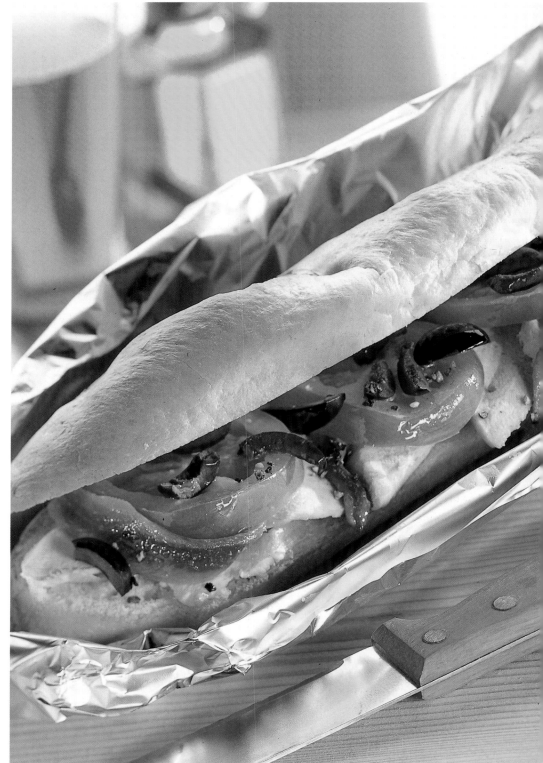

Oaty Chicken Pieces

A very low-fat chicken recipe with a refreshingly light, mustard-spiced sauce, which is ideal for a healthy lunchbox or a light meal with salad.

Serves 4
$^1/_3$ cup rolled oats
1 tbsp chopped fresh rosemary
4 skinless chicken quarters
1 egg white
$^1/_2$ cup reduced fat fromage frais or ricotta cheese
2 tsp wholegrain mustard
salt and pepper
grated carrot salad, to serve

1 Mix together the oats, rosemary, and salt and pepper.

2 Brush each piece of chicken evenly with egg white, then coat in the oat mixture. Place on a cookie sheet and bake in a preheated oven at 400°F for about 40 minutes, or until the juices run clear when the chicken is pierced with the point of a sharp knife.

3 Mix together the fromage frais or ricotta cheese and mustard, season to taste to taste with salt and pepper. Serve with the chicken, hot or cold, with the mustard sauce and a grated carrot salad.

COOK'S VARIATION

Instead of chicken quarters, use skinless, boneless chicken breasts, which are easier to slice. Reduce the cooking time by about 10 minutes and test to check they are done.

Chicken & Cheese Jackets

Use the breasts from a roasted chicken for this delicious, healthy snack.

Serves 4
4 large baking potatoes
8 ounces cooked, boneless chicken breasts
4 scallions
1 cup low-fat soft cheese or Quark
pepper
coleslaw, salad greens, or mixed salad, to serve

1 Scrub the potatoes and prick them all over with a fork. Bake in a preheated oven at 400°F for about 50 minutes, until tender, or cook in a microwave on High power for 12–15 minutes.

2 Dice the chicken, trim, and thickly slice the scallions, and mix them with the low-fat soft cheese or Quark.

3 Cut a cross through the top of each potato and pull slightly apart. Spoon the chicken filling into the potatoes and sprinkle with pepper. Serve immediately with coleslaw, salad greens, or a mixed salad.

COOK'S TIP

Look for Quark in the chill cabinet of the supermarket. It is a low-fat, white, fresh curd cheese made from cow's milk with a delicate, slightly sour flavor.

Cheese & Garlic Drummers

Ideal for informal parties, these tasty chicken drumsticks can be prepared for cooking a day in advance. Instead of baking the chicken drumsticks, you could cook them on the barbecue instead.

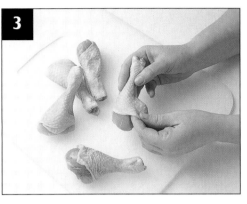

Serves 6
1 tbsp butter
1 garlic clove, crushed
3 tbsp chopped fresh parsley
$\frac{1}{2}$ cup ricotta cheese
4 tbsp grated Parmesan cheese
3 tbsp fresh bread crumbs
12 chicken drumsticks
salt and pepper
lemon slices, to garnish

1 Melt the butter and sauté the garlic gently without browning, stirring, for 1 minute.

2 Remove from the heat and stir in the parsley, the ricotta, Parmesan, bread crumbs and seasoning.

3 Carefully loosen the skin around the chicken drumsticks.

4 Push about 1 tablespoon of the stuffing under the skin of each drumstick. Arrange the drumsticks in a wide roasting pan.

5 Bake in a preheated oven at 375°F for about 45 minutes, until golden. Serve hot or cold, garnished with lemon slices.

COOK'S TIP

Any strongly flavored cheese can be used instead of the Parmesan. Try a sharp Cheddar cheese or use another Italian cheese such as pecorino.

Old English Spicy Chicken Salad

For this simple, refreshing summer salad you can use leftover roast chicken or ready-roasted chicken to save time. Add the dressing just before serving, or the spinach will lose its crispness if left in the dressing for too long.

Serves 4
8 ounces young spinach leaves
3 celery stalks, thinly sliced
$1/2$ cucumber, thinly sliced
2 scallions, thinly sliced
3 tbsp chopped fresh parsley
12 ounces boneless, roast chicken, thinly sliced

DRESSING
1-inch piece fresh ginger root, finely grated
3 tbsp olive oil
1 tbsp white wine vinegar
1 tbsp clear honey
$1/2$ tsp ground cinnamon
salt and pepper
smoked almonds, to garnish (optional)

1 Thoroughly wash the spinach leaves and pat dry with paper towels.

2 Toss the celery, cucumber, and scallions, together with the spinach and parsley in a large bowl.

3 Transfer to serving plates and arrange the chicken over the salad.

4 Combine all the dressing ingredients in a screw-top jar and shake well to mix.

5 Season with salt and pepper to taste, then pour the dressing over the salad. Scatter a few smoked almonds over the salad to garnish, if using.

Sticky Chicken Drummers with Mango Salsa

Delicious served hot or cold, and any leftover chicken can be packed in lunchboxes for a tasty alternative to sandwiches.

Serves 4
8 skinless chicken drumsticks
3 tbsp mango chutney
2 tsp Dijon mustard
2 tsp oil
1 tsp paprika
1 tsp black mustard seeds, roughly crushed
$\frac{1}{2}$ tsp turmeric
2 garlic cloves, chopped
salt and pepper

SALSA
1 mango, diced
1 tomato, finely chopped
$\frac{1}{2}$ red onion, thinly sliced
2 tbsp chopped fresh cilantro

1 Using a small, sharp knife, slash each drumstick three or four times, then place in a roasting pan.

2 Mix together the mango chutney, mustard, oil, spices, and garlic. Season to taste with salt and pepper and spoon the mixture over the chicken drumsticks, turning until they are coated all over with the glaze.

3 Cook in a preheated oven at 400°F, brushing with the glaze several times during cooking, for 40 minutes, until the chicken is well browned and the juices run clear when it is pierced with the point of a sharp knife.

4 Meanwhile, mix together the mango, tomato, onion, and cilantro for the mango salsa. Season to taste and chill until needed.

5 Arrange the chicken drumsticks on a serving plate and serve hot or cold with the mango salsa.

COOK'S VARIATION

Use mild curry powder instead of the turmeric.

Solomongundy

This recipe is ideally suited as a cold platter for a buffet party or a spectacular starter for a special meal.

Serves 4
1 large lettuce
4 chicken breasts, cooked and thinly sliced
8 rollmop herrings and their marinade
6 hard-cooked eggs, quartered
$^2/_3$ cup sliced cooked ham
$2^2/_3$ cups sliced roast beef
$^2/_3$ cup sliced roast lamb
1 cup snow peas, cooked
$^3/_4$ cup seedless black grapes
20 stuffed olives, sliced
12 shallots, boiled
$^1/_2$ cup slivered almonds
$^1/_3$ cup golden raisins
2 oranges
sprig of mint
salt and pepper
crusty bread, to serve

1 Spread out the lettuce leaves on a large oval platter.

2 Arrange the chicken in three sections or lines on the platter.

3 Place the roll mop herrings, egg quarters, ham, beef, and lamb in lines or sections over the remainder of the platter.

4 Use the snow peas, grapes, olive slices, shallots, almonds, and golden raisins to fill in the spaces between the sections.

5 Finely grate the rind from the oranges and sprinkle it over the whole platter. Peel and slice the oranges and add the orange slices and mint sprig to the platter. Season to taste with salt and pepper.

6 Finally, sprinkle with the marinade from the herrings and serve with fresh crusty bread.

COOK'S VARIATION

Should you wish, serve with cold, cooked vegetables, such as sliced beans, baby corn cobs and cooked beets.

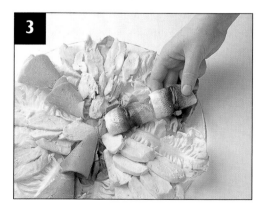

Potted Smoked Chicken

This recipe can be made a few days ahead and kept chilled until needed.
A food processor makes light work of blending the ingredients,
but you can pound by hand for a coarser mixture.

Serves 4–6
2^1/$_2$ cups chopped smoked chicken
pinch of grated nutmeg
pinch of ground mace
^{1}/$_2$ cup butter, softened
2 tbsp port
2 tbsp heavy cream
salt and pepper
slices of brown bread and butter, to serve

1 Place the smoked chicken in a large
bowl with all the ingredients, and
season to taste with salt and pepper.

2 Pound until the mixture is very
smooth or process in a food processor.

3 Transfer the mixture to individual
earthenware pots or one large pot.

4 Cover with buttered wax paper and
weight down with cans or weights.

5 Chill for 4 hours.

6 Remove the paper and cover with
clarified butter (see Cook's Tip).

7 Serve with slices of brown bread
and fresh butter.

COOK'S TIP

To make clarified butter:
Place 1 cup butter in a saucepan
and heat gently, skimming off the
foam as the butter heats.
The sediment sinks to the bottom of
the pan as the butter heats. When
the butter has completely melted,
remove the pan from the heat and
let stand for a least 4 minutes.
Strain the butter through a piece of
cheesecloth into a bowl. Allow the
butter to cool a little before
pouring it over the surface of the
potted chicken.

Chicken & Herb Fritters

These fritters are delicious served with salad greens,
a fresh vegetable salsa, or a chili sauce dip.

Makes 8
1 pound mashed potato, with butter added
1$\frac{1}{3}$ cups chopped, cooked chicken
$\frac{2}{3}$ cup finely chopped cooked ham
1 tbsp mixed herbs
2 eggs, lightly beaten
milk
2 cups fresh brown bread crumbs
oil for shallow frying
salt and pepper

1 In a large bowl, blend the potatoes, chicken, ham, herbs, and 1 egg, and season well with salt and pepper.

2 Shape the mixture into small balls or flat patties.

3 Add a little milk to the second egg.

4 Place the bread crumbs on a plate. Dip the balls in the egg and milk mixture, then roll in the bread crumbs to coat them completely.

5 Heat the cooking oil in a large skillet and fry the fritters, turning frequently until they are golden brown all over.

COOK'S TIP

A mixture of chopped fresh tarragon and parsley makes a fresh and flavorful addition to these fritters.

Chicken Rarebit

A tasty snack that can be served alone or as an
accompaniment to a light, clear soup.

Serves 4
2 cups grated Wensleydale cheese
1¹/₃ cups shredded, cooked chicken
1 tbsp butter
1 tbsp Worcestershire sauce
1 tsp dry English mustard
2 tsp all-purpose flour
4 tbsp mild beer
4 slices of bread
salt and pepper
1 tbsp chopped fresh parsley, to garnish
cherry tomatoes, to serve

1 Place the cheese, chicken, butter, Worcestershire sauce, mustard, flour, and beer in a small saucepan. Mix together and season to taste with salt and pepper.

2 Bring the mixture to a boil over low heat and then remove from the heat immediately.

3 Beat until the mixture becomes creamy in texture. Set aside to cool.

4 Toast the bread on both sides and spread with the chicken mixture. Place under a hot broiler until bubbling and golden brown.

5 Sprinkle with a little parsley and serve with cherry tomatoes.

Open Chicken Sandwiches

These tasty sandwiches are good as a snack on their own or they can
be served as part of a spread.

Serves 6

3 hard-cooked eggs
2 tbsp butter, softened
2 tbsp English mustard
1 tsp anchovy extract
2 cups grated Cheddar cheese
3 cooked, skinless chicken breasts, finely chopped
6 thick slices of bread (crusts removed), buttered, or a large French loaf cut lengthwise, then cut into 6 pieces, buttered
12 slices tomato
12 slices cucumber
pepper

1 Rub the egg yolks through a
strainer and chop the whites. Reserve
the yolk and the white from 1 egg.

2 Mix the remaining egg with the
butter, mustard, and anchovy extract,
and season well with pepper.

3 Mix in the cheese and chicken and
spread the mixture on the bread.

4 Make alternate rows of the egg yolk
and the egg white over the chicken
mixture. Arrange the tomato and
cucumber slices over the rows of egg
and serve.

COOK'S TIP

If you prefer a less hot flavor, use a
milder mustard. Add mayonnaise, if
desired, and garnish with cress.

Coronation Chicken

This classic salad is good as a starter or as part of a buffet.
Mango chutney makes a tasty addition.

Serves 6
4 tbsp olive oil
2 pounds chicken meat, diced
$^2/_3$ cup smoked bacon, diced
12 shallots
2 garlic cloves, crushed
1 tbsp mild curry powder
$1^1/_4$ cups mayonnaise
1 tbsp runny honey
1 tbsp chopped fresh parsley
$^1/_2$ cup seedless black grapes, quartered
pepper

1 Heat the oil in a large skillet add the chicken, bacon, shallots, garlic, and curry powder. Cook slowly for about 15 minutes.

2 With a slotted spoon, spoon the mixture into a clean mixing bowl

3 Allow the mixture to cool completely then season well.

4 Blend the mayonnaise with a little honey, then add the parsley.

5 Toss the chicken in the mixture.

6 Place the mixture in a deep serving dish, garnish with the grapes and serve with cold saffron rice.

Chicken with Pear & Blue Cheese Salad

The combination of chicken, blue cheese, and pears is delicious in this warm salad.

Serves 6
¼ cup olive oil
6 shallots, sliced
1 garlic clove, crushed
2 tbsp chopped fresh tarragon
1 tbsp English mustard
6 skinless, boneless chicken breasts
1 tbsp flour
⅔ cup chicken stock
1 apple, finely diced
1 tbsp chopped walnuts
2 tbsp heavy cream
salt and pepper

SALAD

3½ cups cooked rice
2 large pears, diced
1 cup diced blue cheese
1 red bell pepper, seeded and diced
1 tbsp chopped fresh cilantro
1 tbsp sesame oil

1 Place the olive oil, shallots, garlic, tarragon, and mustard in a deep bowl. Season well and mix the ingredients together thoroughly.

2 Place the chicken in the marinade, cover with plastic wrap, and chill in the refrigerator for about 4 hours.

3 Drain the chicken, reserving the marinade. Quickly fry the chicken in a large, deep nonstick skillet for 4 minutes on both sides. Remove the chicken from the skillet to a warm serving dish. Meanwhile add the marinade to the skillet, bring to a boil, and sprinkle with the flour. Add the chicken stock, apple, and walnuts and

simmer over low heat for 5 minutes. Return the chicken to the skillet, add the cream, and cook for 2 minutes until heated through.

4 Mix the salad ingredients together, place a little on each of six plates, top with a chicken breast, and a spoonful of the sauce. Serve immediately.

Waldorf Summer Chicken Salad

This colorful and healthy dish is a variation of a classic salad.

Serves 4
1 pound red eating apples, diced
3 tbsp fresh lemon juice
$2/3$ cup light mayonnaise
1 head of celery
4 shallots, sliced
1 garlic clove, crushed
$3/4$ cup chopped walnuts
1 pound cooked chicken, cubed
1 Romaine lettuce
pepper
sliced apple and walnuts, to garnish

1 Place the apples in a bowl with the lemon juice and 1 tablespoon of mayonnaise. Set aside for 40 minutes.

2 Slice the celery very thinly.

3 Add the celery with the shallots, garlic, and walnuts to the apple, mix, then add the remaining mayonnaise, and blend thoroughly.

4 Add the chicken, mix, and line a glass salad bowl or serving dish with the lettuce. Pile the chicken salad into the center, sprinkle with pepper, and garnish with apple slices and walnuts.

COOK'S TIP

Instead of the shallots, use scallions for a milder flavor. Trim the scallions and slice finely.

Spiced Chicken & Grape Salad

Tender chicken breast, sweet grapes, and crisp celery coated in a mild curry
mayonnaise make a wonderful al fresco lunch.

Serves 4
1 pound cooked skinless, boneless chicken breasts
2 celery stalks, finely sliced
2 cups black grapes
1/2 cup split almonds, toasted
pinch of paprika
sprigs of fresh cilantro or flat leaf parsley, to garnish

CURRY SAUCE
1/2 cup mayonnaise
1/2 cup ricotta cheese
1 tbsp clear honey
1 tbsp curry paste

1 Cut the chicken into fairly large pieces and transfer to a bowl with the sliced celery.

2 Halve the grapes, remove and discard the pips, and add the grapes to the bowl.

3 To make the curry sauce, mix the mayonnaise, ricotta cheese, honey, and curry paste together until thoroughly blended.

4 Pour the curry sauce over the salad and mix together carefully until all the ingredients are well coated.

5 Transfer the salad to a shallow serving dish and sprinkle with the almonds and paprika. Garnish with the cilantro or flat leaf parsley and serve immediately.

Crunchy-topped Chicken/Spiced Chicken Salad

Cook four chicken pieces together, and serve two hot, topped with a crunchy herb mixture and white sauce, with potatoes or pasta. Use the remainder for a spicy chicken salad.

Serves 2
4 chicken thighs
oil for brushing
garlic powder
$^1/_2$ eating apple, grated coarsely
$1^1/_2$ tbsp dry parsley
and thyme stuffing mix
salt and pepper
pasta shapes, to serve

SAUCE
1 tbsp butter
2 tsp all-purpose flour
5 tbsp milk
2 tbsp dry white wine or stock
$^1/_2$ tsp dried mustard powder
1 tsp capers or chopped cornichons

SPICED CHICKEN SALAD
$^1/_2$ small onion, finely chopped
1 tbsp oil
1 tsp tomato paste
$^1/_2$ tsp curry powder
1 tsp apricot preserve
1 tsp lemon juice
2 tbsp mayonnaise
1 tbsp sour cream
$^3/_4$ cup seedless grapes, halved

1 Place the chicken in an ovenproof dish. Brush with oil, sprinkle with garlic powder, and season with salt and pepper. Cook in a preheated oven at 400°F for 25 minutes.

2 Combine the apple and stuffing mix. Baste the chicken, then spoon the mixture over two of the pieces. Return to the oven for about 10 minutes, until the stuffing is browned and the chicken is cooked.

3 To make the sauce, melt the butter in a pan, stir in the flour, and cook for 1–2 minutes. Gradually add the milk, then the wine or stock. Bring to a boil. Stir in the mustard and capers or cornichons. Serve the chicken with the sauce and pasta shapes.

4 For the salad, sauté the onion in the oil until just colored. Add the tomato paste, curry powder, and apricot preserve, and cook for 1 minute. Cool.

5 Process in a food processor. Beat in the lemon juice, mayonnaise, and sour cream. Season with to taste.

6 Cut the chicken into strips and add to the sauce with the grapes. Mix and chill. Serve with rice and salad.

Roasts & Bakes

The aroma of roasting chicken is always tempting and in this section there are a wealth of delightful recipes. Traditional roast chicken is included, with all the trimmings, as well as many other imaginative treatments. Unusual stuffings add interest—try zucchini and lime, marmalade, or oat and herb stuffing. Many of the recipes in this section exploit the

complementary flavors of chicken and fruits and there are some enticing taste combinations including

cranberries, mango, black cherries, dried apples, peaches, plums, oranges, and mangoes. There are chicken pieces wrapped in bacon, stuffed with ham and cheese, or brushed with honey and mustard. Whole chickens are sprinkled with seeds or cooked with fresh young vegetables. Tasty stuffings are tucked just under the skin to impart flavor and there are boned, easy-to-slice chicken dishes.

Roast Chicken with Cilantro & Garlic

In this recipe, chicken is coated with a fresh-flavored marinade, then roasted.
Try serving it with rice, yogurt, and salad.

Serves 4–6
3 sprigs fresh cilantro, chopped
4 garlic cloves
1/2 tsp salt
1 tsp pepper
4 tbsp lemon juice
4 tbsp olive oil
1 large chicken
pepper

1 Place the chopped cilantro, garlic, salt, pepper, lemon juice, and olive oil in a mortar and pound together with a pestle. Alternatively, process in a food processor.

2 Chill the mixture for 4 hours to allow the flavor to develop.

3 Place the chicken in a roasting pan. Coat generously with the cilantro and garlic mixture.

4 Sprinkle with pepper and roast in a preheated oven at 375°F on a low shelf for about 1 1/2 hours, basting every 20 minutes with the cilantro mixture. If the chicken starts to look brown, cover with foil. Carve into slices and serve.

COOK'S VARIATION

Any fresh herb can be used in this recipe instead of the cilantro. Tarragon or thyme combine well with chicken.

Roast Chicken Breasts with Bacon & Drippings Triangles

Chicken suprêmes have a little bit of the wing bone left which makes them easy to pick up and eat. In this recipe, a tart, fruity sauce perfectly complements the chicken and drippings triangles.

Serves 8
4 tbsp butter
juice of 1 lemon
1 cup red currants or cranberries
1–2 tbsp dark brown sugar
8 chicken suprêmes or breasts
16 slices bacon
thyme
4 tbsp beef drippings
4 slices of bread, cut into triangles
salt and pepper

1 Heat the butter in a saucepan, add the lemon juice and red currants or cranberries, and brown sugar. Season to taste with salt and pepper. Cook for 1 minute and set aside to cool.

2 Meanwhile, season the chicken.

3 Wrap 2 slices of bacon over each breast. Sprinkle with thyme.

4 Wrap each breast in a piece of lightly greased foil and place in a roasting pan. Roast in a preheated oven at 400°F for 15 minutes. Remove the foil and roast for a further 10 minutes.

5 Melt the drippings in a skillet and fry the bread triangles on both sides until golden brown.

6 Arrange the triangles on a large serving plate and top each with a chicken breast. Serve with a spoonful of the fruit sauce.

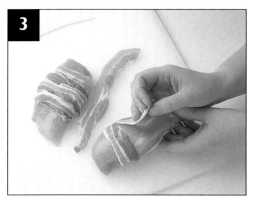

Breast of Chicken with York Ham & Stilton Cheese

Beet is one of the most underrated vegetables, adding flavor and color to numerous dishes. Tender young beets are used in this recipe.

Serves 4
4 chicken suprêmes
8 fresh sage leaves
8 thin slices of York ham
8 ounces Stilton cheese, cut into 8 slices
8 slices bacon
1²/₃ cups chicken stock
2 tbsp port
24 shallots
1 pound baby beets, cooked
1 tbsp cornstarch, blended with a little port
salt and pepper

1 Cut a long slit horizontally along each chicken breast to make a pocket.

2 Insert 2 sage leaves into each pocket and season lightly.

3 Wrap each slice of ham around a slice of cheese and place 2 in each chicken pocket.

4 Carefully wrap enough bacon around each breast to completely cover the pockets containing the cheese and ham.

5 Place the chicken breasts in a casserole dish and pour in the chicken stock and port.

6 Add the shallots, cover with a lid or cooking foil, and braise in a preheated oven at 375°F for about 40 minutes.

7 Carefully transfer each breast to a cutting board and slice through them to create a fan effect. Arrange them on a warm serving dish with the shallots and beets.

8 Put the juices from the casserole into a saucepan and bring to a boil, remove from the heat, and add the cornstarch paste. Return the pan to the heat and gently simmer the sauce for 2 minutes, then pour it over the shallots and beets. Serve immediately.

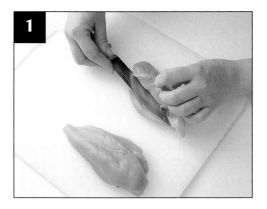

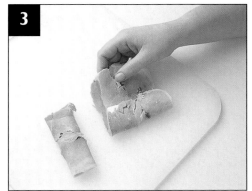

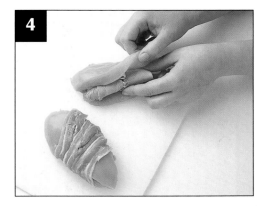

Pot Roast Orange & Sesame Chicken

This colorful, nutritious pot roast could be served for a family meal or for a special dinner.
Add more vegetables if you are feeding a crowd—and if your roasting pot is large enough!

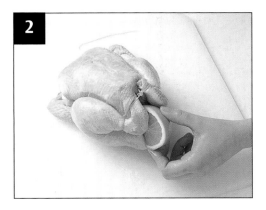

Serves 4
2 tbsp sunflower oil
1 chicken, weighing about 3 pounds
2 large oranges
2 small onions, quartered
2 cups small whole carrots or thin carrots, cut into 2-inch lengths
$^2/_3$ cup orange juice
2 tbsp brandy
2 tbsp sesame seeds
1 tbsp cornstarch
salt and pepper

1 Heat the oil in a large flameproof casserole and fry the chicken, turning occasionally, until evenly browned.

2 Cut one orange in half and place half inside the cavity of the chicken. Place the chicken in a large, deep casserole. Arrange the onions and carrots around the chicken.

3 Season with salt and pepper and pour in the orange juice.

4 Cut the remaining oranges into thin wedges and tuck around the chicken, among the vegetables.

5 Cover and cook in a preheated oven at 350°F, for about 1½ hours, or until there is no trace of pink in the chicken juices when the thigh is pierced with the point of a sharp knife, and the vegetables are tender. Remove the lid and sprinkle with the brandy and sesame seeds, and return to the oven for 10 minutes.

6 To serve, lift the chicken onto a large platter and add the vegetables. Skim any excess fat from the juices. Blend the cornstarch with 1 tablespoon cold water to make a smooth paste, then stir it into the cooking juices and bring to a boil, stirring all the time. Adjust the seasoning to taste, then serve the sauce with the chicken.

Rock Cornish Hens with Dried Fruits

Rock Cornish hens are ideal for a one- or two-portion meal, and cook very easily and quickly for a special dinner. If you are cooking for one and it is not worth putting the oven on, a microwave makes cooking even quicker and more convenient. Use any mixture of dried fruits for a rich fruity flavor and colorful effect.

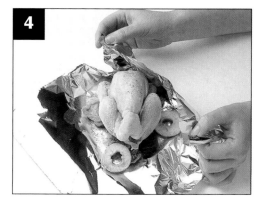

Serves 2
³/₄ cup dried apples, peaches, and prunes
¹/₂ cup boiling water
2 Rock Cornish hens
¹/₃ cup walnut halves
1 tbsp honey
1 tsp ground allspice
1 tbsp walnut oil
salt and pepper
fresh vegetables and new potatoes, to serve

1 Place the dried fruits in a bowl, cover with the boiling water, and set aside to soak for about 30 minutes, until plumped.

2 Cut the Rock Cornish hens in half down the breastbone using a sharp knife, or leave whole.

3 Mix the fruit and any juices with the walnuts, honey, and allspice and divide among two small roasting bags or squares of foil.

4 Brush the Rock Cornish hens with walnut oil and season to taste with salt and pepper, then place them on top of the fruit.

5 Close the roasting bags or fold the foil over to enclose the Rock Cornish hens completely and place on a cookie sheet. Bake in a preheated oven at 375°F for 25–30 minutes, or until the juices run clear when the hen is pierced with the point of sharp knife. To cook in a microwave, use microwave roasting bags and cook on High/100% power for 6–7 minutes each, depending on their size.

6 Serve hot with fresh vegetables and new potatoes.

COOK'S TIP

Alternative dried fruits that could be used in this recipe are cherries, mangoes, or papaya.

Suprême of Chicken with Black Cherries

This recipe is rather time consuming, but it is well worth the effort.
Cherries and chicken make a good flavor combination.

Serves 6
6 large chicken suprêmes
6 black peppercorns, crushed
2 cups pitted fresh black cherries, or canned pitted cherries
12 shallots, sliced
4 slices bacon, chopped
8 juniper berries
4 tbsp port
$^2/_3$ cup red wine
2 tbsp butter
2 tbsp walnut oil
$^1/_4$ cup all-purpose flour
salt and pepper
black cherries and parsley, to garnish

1 Place the chicken in a large deep ovenproof dish. Add the peppercorns, fresh or canned cherries, and their juice, if using, and the shallots.

2 Add the bacon, juniper berries, port, and wine. Season to taste with salt and pepper.

3 Place the chicken and marinade in the refrigerator for 48 hours.

4 Heat the butter and walnut oil in a large skillet. Remove the chicken from the marinade and fry quickly for 4 minutes on each side.

5 Return the chicken to the marinade, reserving the butter, oil, and juices in the pan.

6 Cover the dish with foil and bake in a preheated oven at 350°F for 20 minutes. Transfer the chicken to a warm serving dish. Add the flour to the juices in the skillet and cook for 4 minutes, add the marinade, and bring to a boil, then simmer for 10 minutes until the sauce is thickened and smooth.

7 Pour the sauce over the chicken suprêmes and garnish with black cherries and fresh parsley sprigs or chopped parsley. Serve immediately.

Roast Chicken in Mushroom Sauce

This unusual chicken dish has the flavor of roast chicken, but is finished off in a casserole with an exotic mushroom sauce.

Serves 4
$1/3$ cup butter, softened
1 garlic clove, crushed
1 large chicken
$2^1/4$ cups exotic mushrooms, halved or sliced if large
12 shallots
2 tbsp all-purpose flour
$2/3$ cup brandy
$1^1/4$ cups heavy cream
salt and pepper
1 tbsp chopped fresh parsley, to garnish
wild rice or roast potatoes and Brussels sprouts, to serve

1 Mix together the butter, garlic, and salt and pepper in a bowl.

2 Rub the mixture on the inside and outside of the chicken and set aside for 2 hours.

3 Place in a roasting pan and roast in a preheated oven at 450°F for $1^1/2$ hours, basting every 10 minutes.

4 Remove the chicken from the roasting pan and set aside for 10–15 minutes to cool slightly.

5 Transfer the cooking juices to a saucepan, add the mushrooms and shallots, and cook for 5 minutes. Sprinkle with the flour. Add the brandy, warm slightly, and ignite. Let the flames die down.

6 Add the cream and cook for 3 minutes on very low heat, stirring.

7 Remove and discard the bones from the chicken and cut the meat into bite-size pieces. Place the chicken meat in a casserole, cover with the mushroom sauce, and bake in the oven for a further 12 minutes with the oven temperature reduced to 325°F. Garnish with the parsley and serve immediately with wild rice or roast potatoes, and Brussels sprouts.

Honey & Mustard Baked Chicken

Chicken portions are brushed with a classic combination of honey and mustard, then a crunchy coating of poppy seeds is added.

Serves 4–6
8 skinless chicken portions
4 tbsp butter, melted
4 tbsp mild mustard
4 tbsp clear honey
2 tbsp lemon juice
1 tsp paprika
3 tbsp poppy seeds
salt and pepper
crisp salad, to serve

1 Place the chicken pieces, smooth side down, on a large cookie sheet.

2 Place all the ingredients, except the poppy seeds, in a large bowl and blend together thoroughly.

3 Brush the honey and mustard mixture all over the chicken portions.

4 Bake in the center of a preheated oven at 400°F for 15 minutes.

5 Carefully turn over the chicken pieces and coat the top side of the chicken with the honey and mustard mixture again.

6 Sprinkle the chicken with poppy seeds and return to the oven for a further 15 minutes.

7 Arrange the chicken on a serving dish, pour the cooking juices over them, and serve immediately with a crisp salad.

Californian Chicken

It is better if you have time to bone the chicken completely,
or use chicken breast after removing all the fat and skin.

Serves 4–6
1¹/₂ cups all-purpose flour
1 tsp paprika
1 tsp freeze-dried Italian seasoning
1 tsp freeze-dried tarragon
1 tsp rosemary, finely crushed
2 eggs, beaten
¹/₂ cup milk
1 chicken, weighing about 4 pounds, cut up
seasoned flour
²/₃ cup rapeseed oil
2 bananas, quartered
1 apple, cut into rings,
12 ounce can corn and bell peppers, drained
oil for frying
salt and pepper
watercress and peppercorn or horseradish sauce, to serve

1 Mix together the flour, salt, spices,
and herbs in a large bowl. Make a well
in the center, add the eggs, and blend
together thoroughly.

2 Gradually add the milk, whisking
until very smooth.

3 Coat the chicken pieces with
seasoned flour and then dip them
into the batter to coat thoroughly.
Shake off any excess.

4 Heat the oil in a large skillet. Add
the chicken pieces and fry for about
3 minutes, or until lightly browned all
over. Place the chicken pieces on a
nonstick cookie sheet.

5 Coat the bananas and apple rings in
batter and fry for 2 minutes.

6 Finally, toss the corn and bell
peppers into the leftover batter.

7 Heat a little oil in a skillet. Drop in
spoonfuls of the corn mixture to make
flat patties. Cook for 4 minutes on
each side. Keep warm with the apple
and banana fritters.

8 Bake the chicken in a preheated
oven at 400°F for 25 minutes until the
chicken is tender and golden brown.

9 Arrange the chicken, corn fritters,
and the apple and banana fritters on a
bed of fresh watercress. Serve
immediately with a peppercorn or
horseradish sauce.

Springtime Roast Chicken

Baby chickens are simple to prepare, take about thirty minutes to roast, and can be easily cut in half lengthwise with a sharp knife. One baby chicken makes a substantial serving for each person. This combination of baby vegetables and baby chickens with a tangy low-fat sauce makes a healthy meal.

Serves 4
5 tbsp fresh brown bread crumbs
$^1/_2$ cup ricotta cheese or low-fat crème fraîche
5 tbsp chopped fresh parsley
5 tbsp chopped fresh chives
4 baby chickens
1 tbsp sunflower oil
1$^1/_2$ pounds young spring vegetables, such as carrots, zucchini, sugar snap peas, baby corn cobs, and turnips, cut into small chunks
$^1/_2$ cup boiling chicken stock
2 tsp cornstarch
$^2/_3$ cup dry white wine
salt and pepper

1 Mix together the bread crumbs, one third of the ricotta cheese or crème fraîche, and 2 tablespoons each of parsley and chives. Season to taste with salt and pepper, then spoon the stuffing into the neck ends of the baby chickens. Place the chickens on a rack in a roasting pan, brush with oil, and season well with salt and pepper.

2 Roast in a preheated oven at 425°F for 30–35 minutes, or until the juices run clear when the chickens are pierced with the point of a sharp knife.

3 Place the vegetables in a shallow ovenproof dish in one layer and add half the remaining herbs, together with the stock. Cover and bake for 25–30 minutes, until tender. Lift the chickens onto a serving plate and skim any fat from the juices in the pan. Add the vegetable juices and transfer to a small saucepan.

4 Blend the cornstarch with the wine and whisk into the sauce with the remaining ricotta. Whisk over medium heat until boiling, then add the remaining herbs. Season with salt and pepper to taste. Spoon the sauce over the chickens and serve immediately with the vegetables.

Mediterranean-style Sunday Roast

A roast that is full of Mediterranean flavour. A mixture of feta cheese, rosemary,
and sun-dried tomatoes is stuffed under the chicken skin,
which is then roasted with garlic, new potatoes, and vegetables.

Serves 6
5^1/$_2$ pounds chicken
sprigs of fresh rosemary
^{3}/$_4$ cup coarsely grated feta cheese
2 tbsp sun-dried tomato paste
4 tbsp butter, softened
1 bulb garlic
2 pounds new potatoes, halved if large
1 each red, green, and yellow bell pepper, seeded and cut into chunks
3 zucchini, thinly sliced
2 tbsp olive oil
2 tbsp all-purpose flour
2^1/$_2$ cups chicken stock
salt and pepper

1 Rinse the chicken inside and out with cold water and drain well. Carefully cut between the skin and the top of the breast meat using a small pointed knife. Slide a finger into the slit and carefully enlarge it to form a pocket. Continue until the skin is completely lifted away from both breasts and the top of the legs.

2 Chop the leaves from 3 rosemary stems. Mix with the feta, tomato paste, butter, and pepper, then spoon under the skin. Put the chicken in a large roasting pan, cover with foil, and cook in a preheated oven at 375°F for 40 minutes.

3 Break the garlic bulb into cloves, but do not peel. Add the garlic, potatoes, bell peppers, and zucchini to the chicken.

4 Drizzle with oil, tuck in a few stems of rosemary, and season well. Cook for 50 minutes, remove the foil, and cook for a further 40 minutes, or until the juices run clear when the chicken is pierced with a knife.

5 Transfer the chicken to a serving platter. Place some of the vegetables around the chicken and transfer the remainder to a warm serving dish. Pour the fat from the roasting pan and stir the flour into the remaining juices. Cook for 2 minutes, then gradually stir in the stock. Bring to a boil, stirring until thickened and smooth. Strain into a sauce boat and garnish the chicken with rosemary.

Chicken with Marmalade Stuffing

Marmalade lovers will enjoy this festive recipe. You can use any favorite marmalade, such as lemon or grapefruit.

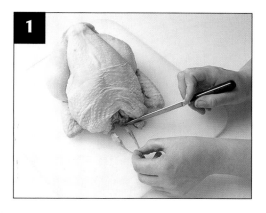

Serves 6
1 chicken, weighing about 5 pounds
bay leaves
2 tbsp marmalade
STUFFING
1 celery stalk, finely chopped
1 small onion, finely chopped
1 tbsp sunflower oil
2 cups fresh whole-wheat bread crumbs
4 tbsp marmalade
2 tbsp chopped fresh parsley
1 egg, beaten
salt and pepper
orange slices and bay leaves or celery leaves, to garnish
SAUCE
2 tsp cornstarch
2 tbsp orange juice
3 tbsp marmalade
$^2/_3$ cup chicken stock
1 medium orange
2 tbsp brandy

1 Lift the neck flap of the chicken and remove the wishbone using a small, sharp knife.

2 Place a sprig of bay leaves inside the body cavity of the bird.

3 To make the stuffing, sauté the celery and onion in the oil to soften. Add the bread crumbs, 3 tablespoons of marmalade, parsley, and egg. Season to taste with salt and pepper. Stuff the neck cavity of the chicken with the mixture. Any extra stuffing may be cooked separately.

4 Place the chicken in a roasting pan and brush lightly with oil. Roast in a preheated oven at 375°F for 2 hours, or until the juices run clear when the chicken is pierced with the point of a knife. Remove from the oven and glaze with the remaining marmalade.

5 Meanwhile, to make the sauce, blend the cornstarch in a pan with the orange juice, then add the marmalade and stock. Heat gently, stirring, until thickened and smooth. Remove from the heat. Cut the segments from the orange, discarding all white pith and membrane. Just before serving, add to the sauce with the brandy and bring to a boil. Serve with the chicken, garnished with orange slices and bay leaves or celery leaves.

Pollo Catalan

The Catalan region of Spain is famous for its wonderful combinations of meat with fruit. Nuts and spices are often added too. In this recipe, peaches lend a touch of sweetness, and pine nuts, cinnamon, and sherry add an unusual twist. Canned peach halves in natural juice make an easy storecupboard alternative.

Serves 6
1 cup fresh brown bread crumbs
¹/₂ cup pine nuts
1 small egg, beaten
4 tbsp chopped fresh thyme or 1 tbsp dried thyme
4 fresh peaches or 8 canned peach halves
1 chicken, weighing about 5¹/₂ pounds
1 tsp ground cinnamon
³/₄ cup Amontillado sherry
4 tbsp heavy cream
salt and pepper

1 Combine the bread crumbs with ¹/₄ cup of the pine nuts, the egg, and fresh or dried thyme.

2 Halve and pit the fresh peaches, and remove the skin if necessary. Dice one peach into small pieces and stir into the bread crumb mixture. Season well with salt and pepper. Spoon the stuffing into the neck cavity of the chicken, securing the skin firmly over it.

3 Place the chicken in a roasting pan and sprinkle the cinnamon all over the skin.

4 Cover loosely with foil and roast in a preheated oven at 375°F for 1 hour, basting occasionally.

5 Remove the foil and spoon the sherry over the chicken. Cook, basting frequently with the sherry juices, for

30 minutes, or until the juices run clear when the chicken is pierced with the point of a sharp knife. Place the remaining peach halves in an ovenproof dish and sprinkle with the remaining pine nuts. Bake in the oven for the final 10 minutes of cooking time.

6 Lift the chicken onto a serving plate and arrange the peaches around it. Skim any fat from the juices, stir in the cream, and heat gently. Serve with the chicken.

Scotch Whisky Roast Chicken

An unusual change from a plain roast, with a distinctly warming Scottish flavor and a delicious oatmeal stuffing.

Serves 6
1 chicken, weighing 4 pounds
1 tbsp heather honey
2 tbsp Scotch whisky
2 tbsp all-purpose flour
1¼ cups chicken stock
green vegetables and sauté potatoes, to serve

STUFFING
1 medium onion, finely chopped
1 celery stalk, thinly sliced
1 tbsp butter or sunflower oil
1 tsp dried thyme
4 tbsp dried oats
4 tbsp chicken stock
salt and pepper

1 To make the stuffing, fry the onion and celery in the butter or oil, stirring over moderate heat until softened and lightly browned.

2 Remove from the heat and stir in the thyme, oats, and stock. Season to taste with salt and pepper.

3 Stuff the neck end of the chicken with the mixture and tuck the neck flap under. Place in a roasting pan, brush lightly with oil, and roast in a preheated oven at 375°F, for about 1 hour.

4 Mix the honey with 1 tablespoon Scotch whisky and brush the mixture over the chicken. Return to the oven for a further 20 minutes, or until the chicken is golden brown and the juices run clear when pierced through the thickest part with the point of a sharp knife.

5 Lift the chicken onto a serving plate. Skim the fat from the juices, stir in the flour over a moderate heat until bubbling, then gradually add the stock and remaining whisky.

6 Bring to a boil, stirring, and simmer for 1 minute. Serve the chicken with the sauce, vegetables, and potatoes.

Gardener's Chicken

Any combination of small, young vegetables can be roasted with the chicken, such as zucchini, leeks, or onions.

Serves 4
4 cups parsnips, peeled and chopped
³/₄ cup carrots, peeled and chopped
¹/₂ cup fresh bread crumbs
¹/₄ tsp grated nutmeg
1 tbsp chopped fresh parsley
1 chicken, weighing about 3 pounds
bunch parsley
¹/₂ onion
2 tbsp butter, softened
4 tbsp olive oil
1 pound new potatoes, scrubbed
1 pound baby carrots washed and trimmed
salt and pepper

1 To make the stuffing, put the parsnips and chopped carrots into a pan, half cover with water, and bring to a boil. Cover and simmer until tender. Drain, then process in a blender or food processor. Transfer the purée to a bowl and let cool.

2 Mix in the bread crumbs, nutmeg, and parsley and season to taste with salt and pepper.

3 Put the stuffing into the neck end of the chicken and push a little under the skin over the breast meat. Secure the flap of skin with a toothpick.

4 Place the bunch of parsley and onion inside the cavity of the chicken, then place the chicken in a large roasting pan.

5 Spread the butter over the skin and season well with salt and pepper, cover with foil, and cook the chicken in a preheated oven at 375°F, for 30 minutes.

6 Meanwhile, heat the oil in a skillet, and lightly brown the potatoes.

7 Transfer the potatoes to the roasting pan and add the baby carrots. Baste the chicken and continue to cook for 1 further hour, basting the chicken and vegetables after 30 minutes. Remove the foil for the last 20 minutes to allow the skin to crisp. Serve immediately.

Festive Apple Chicken

The richly flavored stuffing in this recipe is cooked
under the breast skin of the chicken, so not only is all the flavor sealed in,
but the chicken stays really moist and succulent.

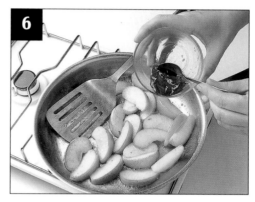

Serves 6
1 chicken, weighing 4 pounds
2 eating apples
1 tbsp butter
1 tbsp red currant jelly
parsley, to garnish
STUFFING
1 tbsp butter
1 small onion, finely chopped
$^3/_4$ cup finely chopped mushrooms,
$^1/_3$ cup finely chopped smoked ham
$^1/_2$ cup fresh bread crumbs
1 tbsp chopped fresh parsley
1 crisp eating apple
1 tbsp lemon juice
oil, for brushing
salt and pepper

1 To make the stuffing, melt the
butter and sauté the onion gently,
stirring until softened but not
browned. Stir in the mushrooms and
cook over a moderate heat for
2–3 minutes. Remove from the heat
and stir in the ham, bread crumbs,
and the chopped parsley.

2 Core the apple, leaving the skin on,
and grate coarsely. Add the stuffing
mixture to the apple with the lemon
juice. Season to taste.

3 Loosen the breast skin of the
chicken and carefully spoon the
stuffing mixture under it, smoothing
it evenly with your hands.

4 Place the chicken in a roasting pan
and brush lightly with oil.

5 Roast the chicken in a preheated
oven at 375°F for 2 hours, or until
there is no trace of pink in the juices
when the chicken is pierced through
the thickest part with the point of a
sharp knife. If the breast starts to
brown too much, cover the chicken
with foil.

6 Core and slice the remaining apples
and sauté in the butter until golden.
Stir in the red currant jelly and warm
through until melted. Serve the
chicken garnished with the apple
slices and parsley.

Chicken with Creamy Zucchini & Lime Stuffing

A cheese stuffing is tucked under the breast skin of the chicken
to give added flavor and moistness to the meat.

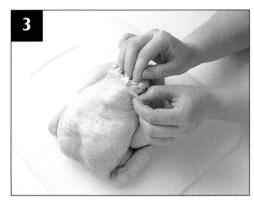

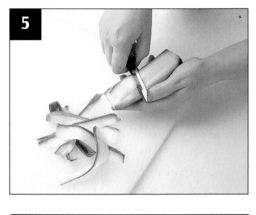

Serves 6
1 chicken, weighing 5 pounds
oil for brushing
8 ounces zucchini
2 tbsp butter
juice of 1 lime
lime slices and shreds of lime rind, to garnish

STUFFING

¹/₂ cup grated zucchini
³/₄ cup medium-fat soft cheese
finely grated rind of 1 lime
2 tbsp fresh bread crumbs
salt and pepper

1 To make the stuffing, trim and coarsely grate the zucchini and mix with the cheese, lime rind, and bread crumbs. Season to taste with salt and pepper.

2 Carefully ease the skin away from the breast of the chicken with the fingertips, taking care not to split it.

3 Push the stuffing under the skin, to cover the breast evenly.

4 Place in a roasting pan, brush with oil,and roast in a preheated oven at 375°F for 2 hours, or until the chicken juices run clear, not pink, when the thickest part is pierced with the point of a sharp knife.

5 Meanwhile, trim the remaining zucchini and cut into long, thin strips with a vegetable peeler or sharp knife. Sauté in the butter and lime juice until just tender, then serve with the chicken. Garnish with lime slices and shreds of lime rind.

COOK'S TIP

For quicker cooking, finely grate the zucchini rather than cutting them into strips.

Cheddar Baked Chicken

Cheese and mustard, and a simple, crispy coating, make a delicious combination for this healthy dish.

Serves 4
1 tbsp milk
2 tbsp prepared English mustard
1 cup grated sharp Cheddar cheese
3 tbsp all-purpose flour
2 tbsp chopped fresh chives
4 skinless, boneless chicken breasts
baked potatoes and fresh vegetables or salad, to serve

1 Mix together the milk and mustard in a bowl. Mix the cheese with the flour and chives on a plate.

2 Dip the chicken into the milk and mustard mixture, brushing with a pastry brush to coat evenly.

3 Dip the chicken breasts into the cheese mixture, pressing to coat them evenly all over.

4 Place the chicken breasts on a cookie sheet and spoon any remaining cheese coating on top.

5 Bake the chicken in a preheated oven at 400°F for 30–35 minutes, until golden brown. Serve the chicken hot, with baked potatoes and fresh vegetables. Alternatively, let cool and serve cold, with a crisp salad.

Feta Chicken with Mountain Herbs

Chicken goes well with most savory herbs, especially during the summer, when fresh herbs are at their best. This combination makes a good partner for tangy feta cheese and sun-ripened tomatoes.

Serves 4
8 skinless, boneless chicken thighs
2 tbsp each chopped fresh thyme, rosemary, and oregano
4 ounces feta cheese
salt and pepper
1 tbsp milk
2 tbsp all-purpose flour
salt and pepper
thyme, rosemary, and oregano, to garnish

TOMATO SAUCE

1 medium onion, roughly chopped
1 garlic clove, crushed
1 tbsp olive oil
4 medium plum tomatoes, quartered
sprig each of thyme, rosemary, and oregano

1 Spread out the chicken thighs on a board, smooth side downward.

2 Divide the herbs among the chicken thighs, then cut the cheese into eight sticks. Place one stick of cheese in the center of each chicken thigh. Season well, then roll up to enclose the cheese.

3 Place the rolls in an ovenproof dish, brush with milk, and dust with flour to coat evenly.

4 Bake in a preheated oven at 375°F for 25–30 minutes, or until golden brown. There should be no pink in the juices when the chicken is pierced with a sharp knife.

5 To make the sauce, cook the onion and garlic in the olive oil, stirring, until softened and just beginning to turn golden brown.

6 Add the tomatoes, reduce the heat, cover tightly, and simmer gently for 15–20 minutes, or until soft.

7 Add the herbs, then transfer to a food processor, and process to a purée. Press through a strainer with the back of a wooden spoon to make a smooth, rich sauce. Season the sauce to taste with salt and pepper. Garnish the chicken with herbs and serve immediately with the sauce.

Honeyed Citrus Chicken

This fat-free recipe is great for summer entertaining served simply with salad greens and new potatoes. If you cut the chicken in half and press it flat, you can roast it in under an hour.

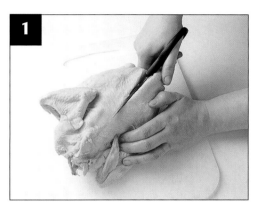  

Serves 4
1 chicken, weighing 4 pounds
salt and pepper
tarragon sprigs, to garnish

MARINADE
1¼ cups orange juice
3 tbsp cider vinegar
3 tbsp clear honey
2 tbsp chopped fresh tarragon
2 oranges, cut into wedges

SAUCE
handful of tarragon sprigs
1 cup reduced fat ricotta cheese
2 tbsp orange juice
1 tsp clear honey
½ cup stuffed olives, chopped

1 Put the chicken on a chopping board with the breast downward. Cut through the bottom part of the carcass using poultry shears or heavy kitchen scissors, making sure not to cut right through to the breast bone below.

2 Rinse the chicken with cold water, drain, and place on a board with the skin side uppermost. Press the chicken flat, then cut off the leg ends.

3 Thread two long wooden skewers through the bird to keep it flat and season the skin with salt and pepper.

4 Put all the marinade ingredients, except the orange wedges, in a nonmetallic dish. Mix, then add the chicken. Cover and chill for 4 hours. Turn the chicken several times.

5 To make the sauce, chop the tarragon, and mix with the sauce ingredients. Season and spoon into a serving dish. Cover and chill.

6 Transfer the chicken and marinade to a roasting pan, open out the chicken and place skin side downward. Tuck the orange wedges around the chicken and roast in a preheated oven at 400°F for 25 minutes.

7 Turn the chicken over and roast for a further 20–30 minutes. Baste until the chicken is browned and the juices run clear when the thickest part of the leg is pierced with a pointed knife. Garnish with tarragon, carve into thin slices, and serve with the sauce.

Chicken with Baby Onions & Green Peas

Pork fat adds a tasty flavor to this dish. If you cannot find fresh garden peas, frozen peas are a good substitute.

Serves 4
1 cup diced pork fat
4 tbsp butter
16 small onions or shallots
2 pounds boneless chicken pieces
$^{1}/_{4}$ cup all-purpose flour
$2^{1}/_{2}$ cups chicken stock
4 cups fresh peas
bouquet garni
salt and pepper

1 Place the diced pork fat in a pan of boiling lightly salted water and simmer for three minutes, then drain, and pat dry.

2 Melt the butter in a large skillet, add the pork and onions, and fry over low heat for 3 minutes, until lightly browned.

3 Remove the pork and onions from the skillet, add the chicken pieces, and brown them all over. Remove them from the skillet and transfer the chicken to a casserole.

4 Add the flour to the skillet and cook, stirring, until it begins to brown, then slowly stir in in the chicken stock.

5 Pour the sauce over the chicken, add the bouquet garni, and cook in a preheated oven at 400°F for 25 minutes.

6 Remove and discard the bouquet garni. Add the onions, pork, and peas and stir to mix well. Return the

casserole to the oven and cook for a further 10 minutes.

7 Place the chicken pieces on a large platter, surround with the pork, peas, and onions, and serve immediately.

COOK'S TIP

If you want to cut down on fat, use lean bacon, cut into small cubes, rather than pork fat.

Traditional Roast Chicken

Roast chicken is an all-time classic which pleases everyone.
Serve it with bread sauce for a delicious meal.

Serves 4–6
1 roasting chicken, weighing about 4 pounds
¹/₄ cup butter
2 pounds potatoes, cut into even-size pieces
4 slices bacon
8 small sausages

STUFFING
1 cup soft white bread crumbs
²/₃ cup ground pork sausagemeat
1 tbsp each chopped mixed fresh herbs and sage

BREAD SAUCE
1¹/₄ cups milk
3 ounces crustless white bread
1 onion, studded with 10 cloves
2 tbsp butter
pinch ground allspice
1 tbsp heavy cream
1 tbsp all-purpose flour
²/₃ cup chicken stock
2–3 tbsp sherry

1 To make the stuffing, mix together the bread crumbs, sausagemeat, mixed herbs, and sage. Spoon the stuffing through the neck end of the bird, using the loose skin to make a full pocket of stuffing.

2 Fasten the flap of skin underneath with string. Put any remaining stuffing in the cavity at the other end. Transfer to a roasting pan and rub with butter. Cover with parchment and bake in a preheated oven for 20 minutes at 400°F. Reduce the oven temperature to 350°F and continue to bake for a further 1 hour 20 minutes. Remove the parchment and baste the chicken.

3 Meanwhile, parboil the potatoes, then drain. Add to the chicken and coat in the fat. Roast for 1 hour.

4 Cut the bacon in half, stretch with a knife, wrap around the sausages, and roast with the chicken for 30 minutes.

5 To make the bread sauce, put all the ingredients in a saucepan together and simmer for 30 minutes. Remove the onion before serving hot.

6 Remove the parchment 15 minutes before the chicken is done, and crisp the skin. Leave the chicken to rest for 20 minutes, in a warm place, while you make the gravy. Serve with the roast potatoes and the sausages, accompanied by the bread sauce.

Golden Chicken with Mango & Cranberries

A partly-boned chicken is easy to slice and serve. If you prefer, stuff in the traditional way at the neck end, and cook any remaining stuffing separately.

Serves 6
1 chicken, weighing about 5 pounds
6 slices smoked bacon
STUFFING
1 ripe mango, diced
¹⁄₄ cup fresh or frozen and thawed cranberries
2 cups bread crumbs
¹⁄₂ tsp ground mace
1 egg, beaten
salt and pepper
GLAZE
¹⁄₂ tsp ground turmeric
2 tsp honey
2 tsp sunflower oil
mango slices and cranberries, to garnish
seasonal vegetables, to serve

1 Dislocate the chicken legs and place the chicken breast side downward.

2 With a sharp knife, cut through the skin along the ridge of the back.

3 Carefully scrape the meat down from the bone on both sides.

4 When you reach the point where the legs and wings join the body, cut through the joints. Work around the ribcage until the carcass can be lifted away. Make six bacon rolls. Mix the mango with the cranberries, bread crumbs, and mace, then bind with egg. Season with salt and pepper.

5 Place the chicken, skin side down, and spoon half the stuffing onto it.

Arrange the bacon rolls down the center, then top with the remaining stuffing. Fold the skin over and tie with string. Turn the chicken over, truss the legs, and tuck the wings underneath. Place in a roasting pan. To make the glaze, mix the turmeric, honey, and oil and brush over the skin.

6 Roast in a preheated oven at 375°F for 1¹⁄₂–2 hours, or until the juices run clear with no pink, when the chicken is pierced with the point of a sharp knife. Cover loosely with foil once the chicken is browned, to prevent overbrowning. Serve the chicken hot with seasonal vegetables.

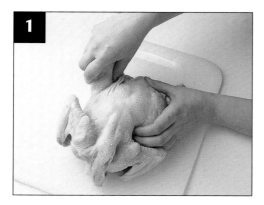

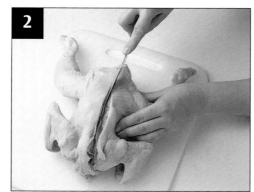

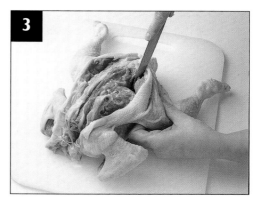

Boned Chicken with Parmesan

It is really very easy to bone a whole chicken, but if you prefer,
you can ask a friendly butcher to do this for you.

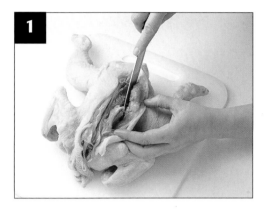

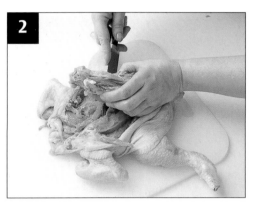

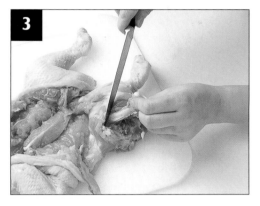

Serves 6
1 chicken, weighing about 5 pounds
8 slices mortadella or salami
2 cups fresh bread crumbs
1 cup freshly grated Parmesan cheese
2 garlic cloves, crushed
6 tbsp chopped fresh basil or parsley
1 egg, beaten
pepper

1 Bone the chicken, keeping the skin intact. Dislocate each leg by breaking it at the thigh joint. Cut down each side of the backbone, taking care not to pierce the breast skin.

2 Pull the backbone clear of the flesh and discard. Remove the ribs, severing any attached flesh with a sharp knife.

3 Scrape away all the flesh from each leg and cut away the bone at the joint with a knife or shears.

4 Use the bones for stock. Lay out the boned chicken on a board, skin side down. Arrange the mortadella slices over the chicken, overlapping slightly.

5 Combine the bread crumbs, Parmesan cheese, garlic, and basil, season well with pepper, and stir in the beaten egg to bind. Pile the mixture down the middle of the boned chicken, roll the meat around it, and tie securely with fine cotton string or trussing thread.

6 Place in a roasting pan and brush lightly with olive oil. Roast in a preheated oven at 400°F for 1½ hours, or until the juices run clear when the chicken is pierced with a sharp knife.

7 Serve hot or cold, in slices, with fresh spring vegetables.

Casseroles

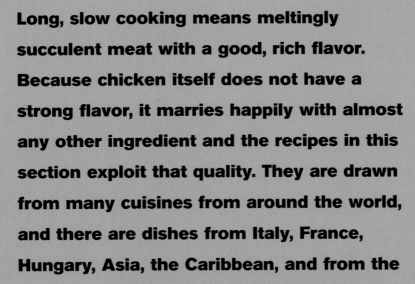

Long, slow cooking means meltingly succulent meat with a good, rich flavor. Because chicken itself does not have a strong flavor, it marries happily with almost any other ingredient and the recipes in this section exploit that quality. They are drawn from many cuisines from around the world, and there are dishes from Italy, France, Hungary, Asia, the Caribbean, and from the United States. French classics include Coq au Vin Blanc, Garlic Chicken Cassoulet, Bourguignonne of Chicken, and

Chicken with 40 Garlic Cloves, a recipe that is not as daunting as it sounds. After cooking, the garlic becomes surprisingly mild and sweet. Chicken also makes a good partner for olives, beans, and rice, and pilaus, and jambalayas are just some of the dishes on offer. Spicy Cajun recipes include Chicken Etouffé and Grillades with Grits.

Chicken Cacciatore

This is a popular Italian classic in which browned chicken quarters
are cooked in a richly flavored sauce of tomatoes and bell peppers.

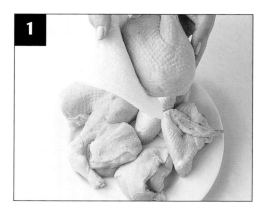

Serves 4
1 roasting chicken, weighing 3 pounds, cut into 6 or 8 serving pieces
1 cup all-purpose flour
3 tbsp olive oil
$^2/_3$ cup dry white wine
1 green bell pepper, seeded and sliced
1 red bell pepper, seeded and sliced
1 carrot, finely chopped
1 celery stalk, finely chopped
1 garlic clove, crushed
7 ounce can chopped tomatoes
salt and pepper

1 Rinse the chicken pieces and pat dry
with paper towels.

2 Lightly dust them with seasoned
flour and brown them in the olive oil
over medium heat. When browned all
over, set the pieces aside.

3 Drain off all but 2 tablespoons of
the fat in the pan, add the wine, and
stir for a few minutes. Add the bell
peppers, carrot, celery, and garlic,
season well with salt and pepper, and
simmer for about 15 minutes.

4 Add the chopped tomatoes and the
chicken pieces to the pan. Cover and
simmer, stirring frequently, for about
30 minutes, until the chicken is
cooked and tender.

5 Check the seasoning, before serving
piping hot.

Chicken with 40 Garlic Cloves

In France, the chicken is served accompanied by slices of bread. Each diner spreads the bread with the softened and sweetened garlic.

Serves 4

1 roasting chicken, weighing about 3 pounds
$1/2$ cup fresh thyme
$1/2$ cup fresh rosemary
$1/2$ cup fresh sage
$1/2$ cup fresh parsley
2 small celery stalks
40 fresh garlic cloves, unpeeled
4 tbsp olive oil
salt and pepper

1 Wash the chicken and pat dry on paper towels. Rub salt into the skin all over.

2 Stuff the cavity with half the fresh herbs, half the celery, and 10 of the garlic cloves.

3 Place the chicken in a roasting pan or earthenware dish, arrange the remaining herbs, celery, and garlic around the chicken, and brush oil all over the skin.

4 Roast in a preheated oven at 400°F for 1½ hours, basting frequently.

5 Transfer the cooked chicken to a warm serving platter and surround with the cloves of garlic. Skim most of the fat from the cooking juices, bring to a boil in the pan, and reduce slightly. Strain into a warmed sauce boat and serve with the chicken.

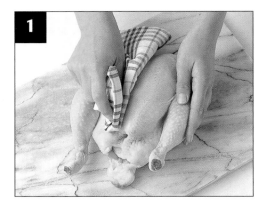

Chicken & Black-eyed Peas

In India and Pakistan, legumes are a valuable source of nourishment in mountainous areas in the winter, when meat is scarce. You could use any variety of legumes in this recipe, but adjust the cooking times accordingly.

Serves 4
1 generous cup dried black-eyed peas, soaked overnight and drained
1 tsp salt
2 onions, chopped
2 garlic cloves, crushed
1 tsp ground turmeric
1 tsp ground cumin
1 chicken, weighing about 2½ pounds, cut up into 8 pieces
1 green bell pepper, seeded and chopped
2 tbsp oil
1-inch piece fresh ginger root, grated
2 tsp coriander seeds
½ tsp fennel seeds
2 tsp garam masala
1 tbsp chopped fresh cilantro, to garnish

1 Put the drained beans into a wok or large skillet, together with the salt, onions, garlic, turmeric, and cumin. Cover with water, bring to a boil, and cook for 15 minutes.

2 Add the chicken and bell pepper to the pan and bring to a boil. Lower the heat and simmer for 30 minutes, until the juices run clear with no trace of pink when the thickest parts of the chicken pieces are pierced with the point of a sharp knife.

3 Heat the oil in a clean wok or skillet and stir-fry the ginger, coriander seeds, and fennel seeds for 30 seconds.

4 Add this mixture to the chicken with the garam masala. Simmer for a further 5 minutes and serve, garnished with fresh cilantro.

Chicken & Chili Bean Pot

This Mexican aromatic chicken dish has a spicy kick. Chicken thighs are not only more economical than breasts, they have much more flavor when cooked in this way.

Serves 4
2 tbsp all-purpose flour
1 tsp chili powder
8 chicken thighs or 4 chicken legs
3 tbsp olive or vegetable oil
2 garlic cloves, crushed
1 large onion, chopped
1 green or red bell pepper, seeded and chopped
1¼ cups chicken stock
2 medium tomatoes, chopped
14 ounce can red kidney beans, drained and rinsed
2 tbsp tomato paste
salt and pepper

5 Return the chicken to the pan. Reduce the heat and simmer, covered, for about 30 minutes, until the chicken is tender. Season with salt and pepper to taste. Transfer to a warm serving dish and serve at once.

COOK'S TIP

Serve this dish with boiled rice or warmed tortillas, with a side dish of sour cream or unsweetened yogurt.

1 Mix together the flour, chili powder, and salt and pepper in a shallow dish. Rinse the chicken, but do not dry. Dip the chicken into the seasoned flour, coating it on all sides and shaking off any excess.

2 Heat the oil in a large, deep skillet or saucepan and add the chicken. Cook over a high heat for about 3–4 minutes, turning the pieces to brown them all over. Remove with a slotted spoon and drain on absorbent paper towels.

3 Add the garlic, onion, and bell pepper to the skillet or pan and sauté gently for about 2–3 minutes, until softened.

4 Add the stock, tomatoes, kidney beans, and tomato paste, stirring well. Bring to a boil.

Chicken with Green Olives

Olives are a popular flavoring for poultry and game in Apulia in Italy, where this recipe originated. In Italy every bit of the bird is used in some way, most often for soups and stock.

Serves 4
4 chicken breasts, part boned
2 tbsp olive oil
2 tbsp butter
1 large onion, finely chopped
2 garlic cloves, crushed
2 red, yellow, or green bell peppers, seeded and cut into large pieces
3 cups sliced or quartered large closed-cup mushrooms
2 small tomatoes, peeled and halved
$2/3$ cup dry white wine
1 cup pitted green olives
4–6 tbsp heavy cream
salt and pepper
chopped flat leaf parsley, to garnish
pasta or tiny new potatoes, to serve

1 Season the chicken with salt and pepper. Heat the oil and butter in a skillet, add the chicken, and fry until browned all over. Remove from the skillet and keep warm.

2 Add the onion and garlic to the skillet and sauté gently until beginning to soften. Add the bell peppers and the mushrooms and continue to cook for a further few minutes.

3 Add the tomatoes and season well with plenty of salt and pepper, and then transfer the vegetable mixture to a casserole. Place the chicken on the bed of vegetables.

4 Add the wine to the skillet and bring to a boil. Pour the wine over the chicken and cover the casserole. Cook in a preheated oven at 350°F for 50 minutes.

5 Add the olives to the chicken, mix lightly, then pour in the cream. Re-cover the casserole and return to the oven for 10–20 minutes, or until the chicken is very tender.

6 Adjust the seasoning and serve the pieces of chicken, surrounded by the vegetables and sauce, with pasta or tiny new potatoes. Sprinkle with parsley to garnish.

Roman Chicken

This Roman dish is equally good cold and could be taken
on a picnic—serve with bread to mop up the juices.

Serves 4
4 tbsp olive oil
6 chicken pieces
4 large mixed red, green, and yellow bell peppers
1 large red onion, sliced
2 garlic cloves, crushed with 1 tsp salt
$^2/_3$ cup pitted green olives
Tomato Sauce (page 138)
$1^1/_4$ cups hot chicken stock
2 sprigs fresh marjoram
salt and pepper

1 Heat half the oil in a flameproof casserole and brown the chicken pieces on all sides. Remove the chicken pieces and set aside.

2 Remove the seeds and the cores from the bell peppers and cut the flesh into strips.

3 Add the remaining oil to the casserole. Sauté the onion gently for 5–7 minutes, until just softened, then add the garlic, and sauté for another minute. Stir in the bell peppers, olives, and tomato sauce and bring to a boil.

4 Return the chicken to the casserole and add the stock and marjoram. Cover the casserole and simmer for about 45 minutes, until the chicken is tender. Season to taste with salt and pepper and serve with crusty bread.

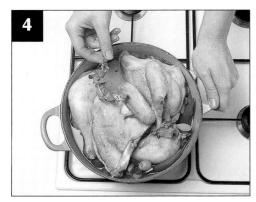

Coq au Vin Blanc

Small pieces of chicken are gently simmered with wine, herbs, bacon, mushrooms, and onions to produce a dish reminiscent of an authentic French meal.

Serves 2
2 chicken leg quarters
4 thick lean bacon slices
2 tbsp oil
8 button onions or 1 large onion, sliced
1 garlic clove, crushed
$^2/_3$ cup dry white wine
$1^1/_4$ cups chicken stock
1 bay leaf
pinch of dried oregano
1 tbsp cornstarch
$^3/_4$ cup tiny button mushrooms, trimmed
salt and pepper
chopped fresh parsley, to garnish
boiled rice or creamed potatoes, to serve

1 Cut each chicken leg into two pieces and season well with salt and pepper. Cut the bacon into ½-inch strips.

2 Heat the oil in a large saucepan. Add the chicken and fry until golden brown all over. Remove from the pan. Add the bacon, onions, and garlic and fry until browned. Drain the fat from the pan.

3 Add the wine, stock, bay leaf, and oregano and season to taste with salt and pepper. Return the chicken to the pan and bring to a boil.

4 Cover the saucepan tightly, lower the heat, and simmer very gently for about 40–50 minutes, or until the chicken is tender and cooked through and the juices run clear when the thickest part is pierced with the point of a sharp knife.

5 Blend the cornstarch with a little cold water to make a smooth paste. Add the cornstarch paste to the saucepan, together with the mushrooms. Bring back to a boil and simmer for a further 5 minutes.

6 Adjust the seasoning and discard the bay leaf. Serve garnished with fresh chopped parsley, with boiled rice or creamed potatoes.

Country Chicken Casserole

Most ceramic casserole dishes can be used with care on the hotplate, but a diffuser can be placed between the heat and the dish—it is usually a double layer of perforated metal holding the dish off the heat. However, you can simply sauté the chicken, then transfer it to an ovenproof dish.

Serves 4
1 chicken, weighing 3 pounds, cut into pieces
flour for dusting
$1/4$ cup butter
1 tsp olive oil
10 pickling onions
3 cloves garlic, unpeeled
1 carrot, diced
1 celery stalk, diced
1 bay leaf
$2/3$ cup diced smoked bacon
about $2^{1}/_{2}$ cups stock
$1^{1}/_{2}$ pounds waxy potatoes, sliced
salt and pepper
green vegetables, to serve

1 Rinse the chicken pieces and pat dry with paper towels. Dust with flour. Melt the butter with the oil in a flameproof casserole over medium-high heat and brown the chicken pieces well all over. Remove from the casserole and set aside.

2 Add the onions, garlic, carrot, celery, bay leaf, and bacon to the casserole. Cook over medium heat for 10 minutes and season well with salt and pepper. Return the chicken to the casserole and pour in the stock. Check the seasoning and adjust if necessary.

3 Arrange the sliced potatoes over the top of the casserole. Cover and simmer for 1 hour.

4 Serve piping hot with a selection of green vegetables.

Chicken with Rice & Peas

This dish, which is also known as chicken pelau, is a national favorite in Trinidad and Tobago. The secret of a good pelau is that it must be brown in color, which is achieved by caramelizing the chicken first.

Serves 6
1 onion, chopped
2 garlic cloves
1 tbsp chopped fresh chives
1 tbsp chopped fresh thyme
2 celery stalks with leaves, chopped
1^1/$_2$ cups water
^{1}/$_2$ fresh coconut, chopped
liquid from 1 fresh coconut
16 ounce can pigeon peas, drained
1 fresh red chili, seeded and cut into strips
2 tbsp groundnut oil
2 tbsp superfine sugar
3 pounds chicken pieces
generous 1 cup long-grain rice, rinsed, and drained
salt and pepper
celery leaves, to garnish

1 Put the onion, garlic, chives, thyme, celery, and 4 tablespoons of the water into a food processor and process until smooth. Or chop the onion and celery very finely, then grind with the garlic and herbs in a mortar with a pestle, gradually mixing in the water. Pour into a pan and set aside.

2 Put the chopped coconut and liquid into the food processor and process to a thick milk, adding water if necessary. Alternatively, finely grate the coconut and mix with the liquid. Add to the onion and celery mixture in the pan.

3 Stir in the pigeon peas and chili strips and cook over low heat for 15 minutes. Season to taste.

4 Put the oil and sugar in a heavy-based casserole and cook over a moderate heat until the sugar begins to caramelize.

5 Add the chicken and cook, turning frequently, for 15–20 minutes, until browned all over.

6 Stir in the coconut mixture, the rice, and remaining water. Bring to a boil, then reduce the heat, cover, and simmer for 20 minutes, until the chicken and rice are tender and the liquid has been absorbed. Garnish with celery leaves and serve.

Chicken & Vegetable Rice

Boneless chicken breasts may be used instead of the drumsticks, in which case slash them diagonally to allow the flavors of the sauce to penetrate.

Serves 4–6
4 chicken drumsticks
3 tbsp mango chutney
1^1/$_2$ tbsp lemon juice
6 tbsp vegetable oil
1–2 tbsp medium or hot curry paste
1^1/$_2$ tsp paprika
1 large onion, chopped
1^1/$_2$ cups button mushrooms
2 carrots, thinly sliced
2 celery stalks, trimmed and thinly sliced
^{1}/$_2$ eggplant, quartered and sliced
2 garlic cloves, crushed
^{1}/$_2$ tsp ground cinnamon
1^1/$_4$ cups long-grain rice
2^1/$_2$ cups chicken stock or water
^{1}/$_2$ cup frozen peas or sliced green beans
^{1}/$_3$ cup raisins
salt and pepper
wedges of hard cooked egg and lemon slices, to garnish (optional)

1 Slash the drumsticks twice on each side, cutting through the skin and deep into the flesh. Mix the chutney with the lemon juice, 1 tablespoon of the oil, the curry paste, and paprika. Brush this over the drumsticks and reserve the remainder.

2 Heat 2 tablespoons of oil in a skillet and fry the drumsticks for about 5 minutes until sealed and golden brown all over.

3 Meanwhile, heat the remaining oil. Add the onion, mushrooms, carrots, celery, eggplant, garlic, and cinnamon, and fry for 1 minute. Stir in the rice and cook for 1 minute, stirring to coat the rice with the oil. Add the stock, the remaining mango chutney mixture, the peas, and raisins. Mix thoroughly and bring to a boil over medium heat.

4 Reduce the heat and add the drumsticks to the mixture, pushing them down into the liquid. Cover and cook gently for 25 minutes, until the liquid is absorbed, the drumsticks are tender, and the rice is cooked.

5 Transfer the rice to a warm serving plate and arrange the drumsticks around it. Garnish the dish with wedges of hard-cooked egg and lemon slices, if using.

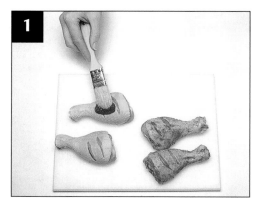

Jambalaya

Jambalaya, a New Orleans version of paella, dates back to the eighteenth century, when it was served as slave food. Today, this hearty rice dish can contain any number of meats, such as chicken, duck, ham, or sausage.

Serves 4
1/4 cup butter
2 onions, chopped
2 garlic cloves, crushed
5 celery stalks, chopped
1 red bell pepper, chopped
1 green bell pepper, chopped
1 tsp Cajun Spice Mixture (page 199)
1 cup long-grain rice
14 ounce can tomatoes, drained and chopped
1 pound cooked assorted meats (chicken, duck, ham, or sausage), sliced or diced
1 cup vegetable stock or white wine
1 tsp salt
parsley sprigs, to garnish

1 Melt the butter in a large, heavy-based pan. Add the onions, garlic, celery, bell peppers, and spice mixture and mix well.

2 Add the rice and stir well to coat the grains in the butter mixture.

3 Add the tomatoes, meats, stock or wine, and salt to taste. Bring to a boil, stirring well.

4 Reduce the heat, cover, and simmer for about 15 minutes, or until the rice is cooked and fluffy and has absorbed all the liquid. If the mixture seems to be too dry then add a little boiling water, tablespoon by tablespoon, toward the end of the cooking time.

5 Serve the jambalaya on warm plates, garnished with parsley.

Baton Rouge Chicken Gumbo

Everyone in the state of Louisiana has their own favorite gumbo recipe.
This one uses chicken with shrimp, okra, and a little belly of pork:
a recipe that is hard to improve upon.

Serves 4–6
2 tbsp butter
1 tbsp corn oil
$\frac{1}{4}$ cup all-purpose flour
3 ounces belly pork, sliced
1 large onion, sliced
2 celery stalks, chopped
1 pound okra, trimmed and sliced
14 ounce can peeled tomatoes
2 garlic cloves, crushed
$4\frac{1}{2}$ cups chicken stock or water
8 ounces peeled shrimp
1 pound cooked chicken, skinned and cut into bite-size pieces
1 tsp Tabasco sauce
3 cups hot cooked rice, to serve

1 Heat the butter and oil in a small, heavy-based pan. Add the flour and cook, stirring frequently, over a low heat until the roux turns a rich brown color. Set aside.

2 Meanwhile, gently fry the pork slices in a large, heavy-based skillet, without extra fat, until they are golden brown on all sides and the fat has been rendered. Add the sliced onion and celery, and cook, stirring frequently, for a further 5 minutes.

3 Stir in the slice okra and sauté gently, stirring occasionally, for a further 3 minutes. Stir in the tomatoes and garlic and simmer over low heat for 15 minutes.

4 Gradually add the stock to the browned roux, mixing and blending well, then add to the okra mixture. Cover and simmer for 1 hour.

5 Add the shrimp and chicken to the okra mixture, cook for a further 5 minutes, until the chicken is thoroughly reheated. Stir in the Tabasco sauce.

6 Spoon the gumbo into individual serving bowls and top with a scoop of hot cooked rice. Serve at once.

Chicken Etouffé

Etouffé means smothered and is a popular way of presenting food in Cajun cuisine. Here, strips of chicken and vegetables are smothered in a thickened dark sauce flavored with basil.

Serves 4–6
¼ cup butter
1 small onion, chopped
1 celery stalk, chopped
1 small green bell pepper, seeded and chopped
1 red bell pepper, seeded and chopped
1 small red chili, seeded and finely chopped
1 tsp Cajun Spice Mixture (see page 199)
1 tsp chopped fresh basil
2 tbsp vegetable oil
2 tbsp flour
2 cups rich chicken stock
1 pound skinless, boneless chicken breasts, cut into strips or bite-size pieces
4 scallions, chopped
salt
rice or couscous, to serve

1 Melt the butter in a large, heavy-based pan. Add the onion, celery, green and red bell peppers, and chili and cook over low heat for about 5 minutes, until softened.

2 Add the Cajun spice mixture, basil, and salt to taste. Cook for a further 2 minutes.

3 Meanwhile, heat the oil in a pan, add the flour, and cook over low heat until a rich red/brown roux is formed. Whisk constantly to prevent the roux from scorching and becoming bitter.

4 Gradually add the stock and whisk well to make a smooth, thickened sauce. Pour the sauce over the vegetable mixture and simmer for about 15 minutes.

5 Add the chicken strips and the scallions and cook, stirring occasionally, for a further 10 minutes, until the chicken is cooked through and tender.

6 Serve with cooked long-grain rice or freshly cooked, fluffy couscous.

Grillades with Grits

Grillades is a Cajun meat and vegetable stew in a thick gravy. It is considered to be Bayou breakfast food and would always be served with grits, a kind of creamy cereal made from corn.

Serves 6
4 tbsp olive oil
2 pounds skinless, boneless chicken breasts, cut into 3 × 4 inch strips
$^1/_2$ cup all-purpose flour
3 onions, chopped
2 green bell peppers, seeded and chopped
4 celery stalks, finely chopped
1 garlic clove, crushed
3 medium ripe tomatoes, peeled, seeded, and chopped
2 tbsp tomato paste
1 tsp chopped fresh thyme
$^1/_2$–1 tsp Tabasco sauce
$1^1/_2$ tsp paprika
$^1/_4$ tsp cayenne pepper
1 tsp salt
$^2/_3$ cup vegetable stock
$^2/_3$ cup white wine
grits hominy or couscous, to serve

1 Heat the olive oil in a heavy-based skillet. Add the chicken strips and fry quickly on both sides, stirring frequently, until no longer pink and the meat is sealed and light brown all over. Remove with slotted spoon and set aside.

2 Add the flour to the juices in the skillet and mix well, stirring until the flour is completely absorbed by the juices. Cook over low heat, stirring constantly, until the roux changes to a rich brown color.

3 Add the onions, bell peppers, celery, and garlic and mix. Cover and cook over low heat for 15 minutes.

4 Return the chicken to the pan with the tomatoes, tomato paste, thyme, Tabasco sauce, paprika, cayenne, salt, stock, and wine, mixing well.

5 Cover and simmer gently for a further 40–45 minutes, or until the chicken and vegetables are cooked through and tender.

6 Transfer to a warm serving dish and serve hot with grits or couscous.

Bourguignon of Chicken

A recipe based on a classic French dish. Use a good quality wine
when making this casserole.

Serves 4–6

4 tbsp sunflower oil

1³/₄ pounds skinless, boneless
chicken, diced

3 cups button mushrooms

²/₃ cup diced smoked bacon

16 shallots

2 garlic cloves, crushed

1 tbsp all-purpose flour

²/₃ cup white Burgundy wine

²/₃ cup chicken stock

1 bouquet garni (1 bay leaf, sprig of
thyme, celery stalk, sprig of
parsley, and sprig of sage
tied with string)

salt and pepper

deep-fried croûtons,
to serve

1 Heat the sunflower oil in an
ovenproof casserole and brown the
chicken all over. Remove from the
casserole with a slotted spoon.

2 Add the mushrooms, bacon,
shallots, and garlic to the casserole
and cook for 4 minutes.

3 Return the chicken to the casserole
and sprinkle with flour. Cook for a
further 2 minutes.

4 Add the wine and stock and stir
until boiling. Add the bouquet garni
and season well with salt and pepper.

5 Cover the casserole and bake in the
center of a preheated oven at 300°F
for 1½ hours. Remove and discard the
bouquet garni.

6 Deep fry some croûtons (about
8 large ones) in beef dripping and
serve with the bourguignon.

COOK'S TIP

A good quality red wine can be
used instead of the white wine to
produce a rich, glossy red sauce.

Spiced Chicken Casserole

Spices, herbs, fruit, nuts, and vegetables are combined to make an appealing casserole with lots of flavor.

Serves 4–6
3 tbsp olive oil
1³/₄ pounds chicken meat, sliced
10 shallots or pickling onions
3 carrots, chopped
¹/₂ cup chestnuts, sliced
¹/₂ cup slivered almonds, toasted
1 tsp freshly grated nutmeg
3 tsp ground cinnamon
1¹/₄ cups white wine
1¹/₄ cups chicken stock
³/₄ cup white wine vinegar
1 tbsp chopped fresh tarragon
1 tbsp chopped fresh flat leaf parsley
1 tbsp chopped fresh thyme
grated rind of 1 orange
1 tbsp dark brown sugar
³/₄ cup seedless black grapes, halved
sea salt and pepper
fresh herbs, to garnish
wild rice or puréed potato, to serve

1 Heat the olive oil in a large saucepan and fry the chicken, shallots, and carrots for about 6 minutes, until the chicken is browned all over.

2 Add the remaining ingredients, except the grapes, and simmer over low heat for 2 hours, until the meat is very tender.

3 Add the black grapes just before serving and heat through. Garnish with herbs and serve with wild rice or puréed potato.

Hungarian Chicken Goulash

Goulash is traditionally made with beef, but this recipe successfully uses chicken instead. To reduce fat, use a reduced fat cream in place of the sour cream.

Serves 6
1³/₄ pounds chicken meat, diced
¹/₂ cup flour, seasoned with
1 tsp paprika, salt, and pepper
2 tbsp olive oil
2 tbsp butter
1 onion, sliced
24 shallots, peeled
1 each red and green bell pepper, seeded, and chopped
1 tbsp paprika
1 tsp rosemary, crushed
4 tbsp tomato paste
1¹/₄ cups chicken stock
²/₃ cup claret
14 ounce can chopped tomatoes
²/₃ cup sour cream
1 tbsp chopped fresh parsley, to garnish
crusty bread and salad, to serve

1 Toss the meat in the seasoned flour until coated all over. Shake off any excess flour.

2 Heat the oil and butter in a flameproof casserole and fry the onion, shallots, and bell peppers, stirring occasionally, for 3 minutes.

3 Add the chicken and cook for a further 4 minutes.

4 Sprinkle with the paprika and rosemary.

5 Add the tomato paste, stock, claret, and chopped tomatoes, cover, and cook in the center of a preheated oven at 325°F for 1¹/₂ hours.

6 Remove the casserole from the oven, let stand for 4 minutes, then add the sour cream, and garnish with chopped parsley.

7 Serve with chunks of bread and a side salad.

COOK'S VARIATION

Serve the goulash with buttered ribbon noodles instead of bread. For an authentic touch, try a Hungarian red wine instead of the claret.

Chicken with Shallots in Mushroom & Ginger Sauce

This recipe has an Eastern flavor, which can be further enhanced with chopped scallions, cinnamon, and lemon grass.

Serves 6–8
6 tbsp sesame oil
1³/₄ pounds chicken meat
¹/₂ cup seasoned flour
32 shallots, sliced
6 cups exotic mushrooms, roughly chopped
1¹/₄ cups chicken stock
2 tbsp Worcestershire sauce
1 tbsp honey
2 tbsp grated fresh root ginger
²/₃ cup unsweetened yogurt
salt and pepper
flat leaf parsley, to garnish
mixed wild and white rice, to serve

1 Heat the oil in a large skillet. Coat the chicken in the seasoned flour and cook for about 4 minutes, until browned all over. Transfer to a large deep casserole.

2 Gently sauté the shallots and mushrooms in the cooking juices in the skillet.

3 Add the stock, Worcestershire sauce, honey, and fresh ginger, then season to taste with salt and pepper.

4 Pour the mixture over the chicken, and cover the casserole with a lid or cooking foil.

5 Cook in the center of a preheated oven at 300°F for 1¹/₂ hours, until the meat is very tender. Add the yogurt and cook for a further 10 minutes. Garnish with parsley and serve with a mixture of wild rice and white rice.

Fricassée of Chicken in Lime Sauce

The addition of lime juice and lime rind adds a delicious tangy
flavor to this chicken stew.

Serves 4
2 tbsp oil
1 large chicken, cut into small portions
$1/2$ cup seasoned flour
1 pound baby onions or shallots, sliced
1 each green and red bell pepper, seeded and thinly sliced
$2/3$ cup chicken stock
juice and rind of 2 limes
2 chilies, chopped
2 tbsp oyster sauce
1 tsp Worcestershire sauce
salt and pepper

1 Heat the oil in a large, heavy-based skillet. Coat the chicken pieces in the seasoned flour and shake off the excess. Add to the skillet and fry, turning frequently, for about 4 minutes, until browned all over.

2 Transfer the chicken to a large, deep casserole and sprinkle with the sliced onions.

3 Gently sauté the bell peppers in the juices in the skillet.

4 Add the chicken stock, lime juice and rind and cook for a further 5 minutes.

5 Add the chilies, oyster sauce, and Worcestershire sauce. Season to taste with salt and pepper.

6 Pour the peppers and juices over the chicken and onions.

7 Cover the casserole with a lid or cooking foil.

8 Cook in the center of a preheated oven at 375°F for 1½ hours, until the chicken is very tender, then serve.

COOK'S TIP

Try this casserole with a cheese biscuit topping. About 30 minutes before the end of cooking time, simply top with rounds cut from cheese biscuit pastry.

Brittany Chicken Casserole

A hearty, one-dish meal that would make a substantial lunch or supper.

Serves 6

2½ cups beans, such as small navy beans, soaked overnight and drained
2 tbsp butter
2 tbsp olive oil
3 slices bacon, chopped
1¾ pounds chicken pieces
1 tbsp all-purpose flour
1¼ cups cider
⅔ cup chicken stock
14 shallots
2 tbsp honey, warmed
8 ounces ready-cooked beets
salt and pepper

1 Cook the beans in lightly salted boiling water for about 25 minutes.

2 Meanwhile, heat the butter and olive oil in a flameproof casserole, add the bacon and chicken, and cook, stirring and turning frequently, for 5 minutes.

3 Sprinkle with flour, then add the cider and chicken stock. Mix thoroughly, season to taste with salt and pepper, and bring to a boil.

4 Drain the beans, add them to the casserole, and mix thoroughly, but gently. Cover tightly with a lid or cooking foil, and bake in the center of a preheated oven at 325°F for 2 hours.

5 About 15 minutes before the end of cooking time, remove the lid or cooking foil from the casserole.

6 Gently cook the shallots and honey together in a skillet for 5 minutes.

7 Add the shallots and cooked beets to the casserole and return to the oven for a further 15 minutes. Serve hot.

COOK'S TIP

To save time, use canned small navy beans instead of dried. Drain and rinse before adding to the chicken.

Chicken Madeira "French-style"

Madeira adds a rich, full flavor to this casserole dish.

Serves 8
2 tbsp butter
20 baby onions
1 1/2 cups sliced carrots
1 1/2 cups chopped bacon
3 cups button mushrooms
1 chicken, weighing about 3 pounds
2 cups white wine
1/4 cup seasoned flour
scant 2 cups chicken stock
bouquet garni
2/3 cup Madeira
salt and pepper
mashed potato or pasta, to serve

1 Heat the butter in a large skillet and sauté the onions, carrots, bacon, and mushrooms for 3 minutes. Transfer to a large casserole dish.

2 Add the chicken to the skillet and fry, stirring frequently, until brown all over. Transfer to the casserole dish with the vegetables and bacon.

3 Add the wine and cook until the liquid is almost completely reduced.

4 Sprinkle with the seasoned flour.

5 Add the chicken stock, salt and pepper, and the bouquet garni. Cover and cook for 2 hours. About 30 minutes before the end of cooking time, add the Madeira and continue to cook uncovered.

6 Carve the chicken and serve with mashed potato or pasta.

Garlic Chicken Cassoulet

This is a cassoulet with a twist—it is made with chicken instead of duck and lamb.
Save time by using canned beans, such as borlotti or cannellini beans,
which are both good in this dish.

Serves 4
4 tbsp sunflower oil
1³/₄ pounds chicken meat, chopped
3 cups sliced mushrooms
16 shallots
6 garlic cloves, crushed
1 tbsp all-purpose flour
1 cup white wine
1 cup chicken stock
1 bouquet garni (1 bay leaf, sprig thyme, celery stalk, sprig parsley, and sage tied together with string)
14 ounce can borlotti beans, drained and rinsed
salt and pepper

1 Heat the sunflower oil in an ovenproof casserole and fry the chicken until browned all over. Remove from the casserole with a slotted spoon.

2 Add the mushrooms, shallots, and garlic to the fat in the casserole and cook for 4 minutes.

3 Return the chicken to the casserole and sprinkle with the flour, then cook for a further 2 minutes.

4 Add the wine and stock, stir until boiling, then add the bouquet garni. Season well with salt and pepper.

5 Stir in the borlotti beans.

6 Cover tightly and cook in the center of a preheated oven at 300°F for 2 hours, until tender. Remove the bouquet garni and serve at once.

Country Chicken Braise with Rosemary Dumplings

Root vegetables are always cheap and nutritious, and combined with chicken, they make tasty and economical casseroles.

Serves 4
4 chicken quarters
2 tbsp sunflower oil
2 medium leeks
1 cup chopped carrots
2 cups chopped parsnips
2 small turnips, chopped
2$^{1}/_{2}$ cups chicken stock
3 tbsp Worcestershire sauce
2 sprigs fresh rosemary
salt and pepper
DUMPLINGS
1$^{3}/_{4}$ cups self-rising flour
$^{3}/_{4}$ cup shredded suet
1 tbsp chopped rosemary leaves
cold water, to mix

1 Remove the skin from the chicken if desired. Heat the oil in a large, flameproof casserole or heavy pan and fry the chicken, turning frequently, until golden. Remove from the pan. Drain off the excess fat.

2 Trim and slice the leeks. Add the leeks, carrots, parsnips, and turnips to the casserole and cook for 5 minutes, until lightly colored. Return the chicken to the pan.

3 Add the stock, Worcestershire sauce, rosemary, and salt and pepper to taste, then bring to a boil.

4 Reduce the heat, cover, and simmer gently for about 50 minutes, or until the chicken juices run clear when the chicken is pierced with the point of a sharp knife.

5 To make the dumplings, combine the flour, suet, and rosemary leaves with salt and pepper in a bowl. Stir in just enough cold water to bind to a firm dough.

6 Form into 8 small balls and place on top of the chicken and vegetables. Cover and simmer for a further 10–12 minutes, until the dumplings are well risen. Serve hot.

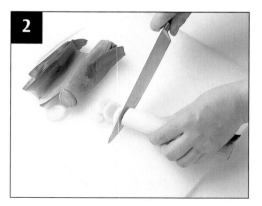

Rustic Chicken & Orange Pot

Low in fat and high in fiber, this colorful casserole
makes a healthy and hearty meal.

Serves 4
8 skinless chicken drumsticks
1 tbsp whole-wheat flour
1 tbsp olive oil
2 medium red onions
1 garlic clove, crushed
1 tsp fennel seeds
1 bay leaf
finely grated rind and juice of 1 small orange
14 ounce can chopped tomatoes
14 ounce can cannellini or small navy beans, drained and rinsed
salt and black pepper

TOPPING
3 thick slices whole-wheat bread
2 tsp olive oil

1 Toss the chicken drumsticks in the whole-wheat flour to coat evenly. Heat the oil in a nonstick or heavy-based skillet, add the chicken, and fry over fairly high heat, turning often until golden brown. Transfer to a large casserole.

2 Using a sharp knife, slice the red onions into thin wedges. Add to the skillet and cook for a few minutes, stirring occasionally, until lightly browned. Stir in the garlic, then transfer the onions and garlic to the casserole.

3 Add the fennel seeds, bay leaf, orange rind and juice, tomatoes, and beans. Season to taste with salt and pepper.

4 Cover tightly and cook in a preheated oven at 375°F for 30–35 minutes, until the chicken juices are clear and not pink when the chicken is pierced through the thickest part with the point of a sharp knife.

5 For the topping, cut the bread into small dice and toss in the oil. Remove the lid from the casserole and top with the bread cubes. Bake for a further 15–20 minutes, until the bread is golden and crisp. Serve hot.

Rich Mediterranean Chicken Casserole

A colorful casserole packed with sunshine flavors from the Mediterranean. Sun-dried tomatoes add a wonderful richness and you need very few to make this dish really special.

Serves 4
8 chicken thighs
2 tbsp olive oil
1 medium red onion, sliced
2 garlic cloves, crushed
1 large red bell pepper, seeded and thickly sliced
thinly pared rind and juice of 1 small orange
$^{1}/_{2}$ cup chicken stock
14 ounce can chopped tomatoes
$^{1}/_{2}$ cup sun-dried tomatoes, thinly sliced
1 tbsp chopped fresh thyme
$^{1}/_{2}$ cup pitted black olives
salt and pepper
thyme sprigs and orange rind, to garnish
crusty bread, to serve

1 In a large heavy-based or nonstick skillet, fry the chicken thighs without fat over a fairly high heat, turning occasionally, until sealed and golden brown all over. Drain off any excess fat from the chicken and transfer to a flameproof casserole.

2 Fry the onion, garlic, and bell pepper in the skillet over moderate heat for 3–4 minutes. Transfer the vegetables to the casserole.

3 Add the orange rind and juice, chicken stock, canned tomatoes, and sun-dried tomatoes.

4 Bring to a boil, then cover with a lid, and simmer very gently over low heat, stirring occasionally, for about 1 hour. Add the thyme and olives, then taste, and adjust the seasoning if necessary.

5 Scatter orange rind and thyme over the casserole to garnish, and serve with crusty bread.

Old English Chicken Stewed in Beer

A slow-cooked, old-fashioned stew to warm up a wintry day.
The rarebit toasts are a perfect accompaniment to soak up the rich juices,
but if desired, serve the stew with baked potatoes.

Serves 4–6
4 large, skinless chicken thighs
2 tbsp all-purpose flour
2 tbsp English mustard powder
2 tbsp sunflower oil
1 tbsp butter
4 small onions
2$\frac{1}{2}$ cups beer
2 tbsp Worcestershire sauce
3 tbsp chopped fresh sage leaves
salt and pepper
green vegetables and new potatoes, to serve

FOR THE RAREBIT TOASTS

$\frac{1}{2}$ cup grated sharp Cheddar cheese
1 tsp English mustard powder
1 tsp all-purpose flour
1 tsp Worcestershire sauce
1 tbsp beer
2 slices whole-wheat toast

1 Trim any fat from the chicken and toss the meat in the flour and mustard to coat. Heat the oil and butter in a flameproof casserole and fry the chicken over fairly high heat until golden. Remove and keep hot.

2 Cut the onions into wedges and fry quickly until golden. Add the chicken, beer, and Worcestershire sauce. Season to taste with salt and pepper. Bring to a boil, cover, and simmer very gently for about 1½ hours, until the chicken is very tender.

3 Meanwhile, make the rarebit toasts: mix the cheese with the mustard, flour, Worcestershire sauce, and beer. Spread over the toasts and place under a hot broiler for about 1 minute, until melted and golden. Cut into triangles.

4 Stir the sage into the chicken stew, bring to a boil, and serve with the rarebit toasts, green vegetables, and new potatoes.

Jamaican Hot Pot

A tasty way to make chicken joints go a long way, this hearty casserole, spiced with the warm, subtle flavor of ginger, is a good choice for a Halloween party. If squash or pumpkin is not available, rutabaga makes a good substitute.

Serves 4
2 tsp sunflower oil
4 chicken drumsticks
4 chicken thighs
1 medium onion
1$^1/_2$ pounds piece squash or pumpkin, diced
1 green bell pepper, sliced
1-inch piece fresh ginger root, finely chopped
14 ounce can chopped tomatoes
1$^1/_4$ cups chicken stock
$^1/_4$ cup split lentils
garlic salt
cayenne pepper
12 ounce can corn cobs, drained
crusty bread, to serve

1 Heat the oil in a large flameproof casserole and fry the chicken joints, turning frequently, until golden.

2 Peel and slice the onion.

3 Peel and slice the squash or pumpkin.

4 Seed and slice the bell pepper.

5 Drain excess fat from the pan and add the onion, pumpkin, and pepper. Gently fry for a few minutes until lightly browned. Add the ginger, tomatoes, stock, and lentils. Season lightly with garlic salt and cayenne.

6 Cover and cook in a preheated oven, at 375°F for about 1 hour, until the vegetables are tender and the juices from the chicken run clear when the thickest part is pierced with the point of a sharp knife. Add the corn and cook for a further 5 minutes. Season to taste and serve immediately with crusty bread.

COOK'S VARIATION

If you can't find fresh ginger root, add 1 teaspoon allspice for a warm, fragrant aroma.

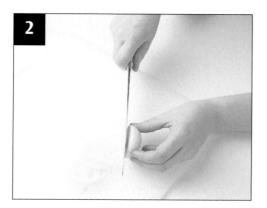

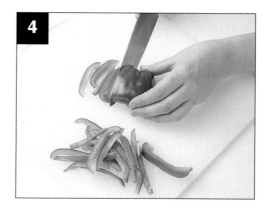

Springtime Chicken Cobbler

Fresh spring vegetables are the basis of this colorful casserole, which is topped with hearty whole-wheat dumplings for a complete, healthy family meal. Vary the vegetables depending on what is available.

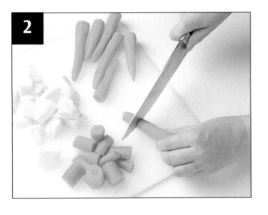

Serves 4
8 skinless chicken drumsticks
1 tbsp oil
1 small onion, sliced
1½ cups baby carrots
2 baby turnips
1 cup fava beans or peas
1 tsp cornstarch
1¼ cups chicken stock
2 bay leaves
salt and pepper

COBBLER TOPPING

2 cups whole-wheat all-purpose flour
2 tsp baking powder
2 tbsp sunflower soft margarine
2 tsp dry wholegrain mustard
½ cup Cheddar cheese, grated
skim milk, to mix
sesame seeds, to sprinkle

1 Fry the chicken in the oil, turning , until golden brown. Drain well and place in an ovenproof casserole. Sauté the onion for 2–3 minutes, to soften.

2 Wash and trim the carrots and turnips and cut into equal-size pieces. Add to the casserole with the onions and beans or peas.

3 Blend the cornstarch with a little of the stock, then stir in the rest, and heat gently, stirring until boiling. Pour into the casserole and add the bay leaves, salt and pepper.

4 Cover tightly and bake in a preheated oven at 400°F for

50–60 minutes, or until the juices run clear when the chicken is pierced with the point of a sharp knife.

5 For the topping, sift the flour and baking powder. Mix in the margarine with a fork. Stir in the mustard, cheese and enough milk to mix to a fairly soft dough.

6 Roll out and cut 16 rounds with a 1½-inch cutter. Uncover the casserole, arrange the biscuit rounds on top, then brush with milk, and sprinkle with sesame seeds. Bake in the oven for 20 minutes, or until the topping is golden and firm.

Country Chicken Hot-Pot

There are many regional versions of hot-pot, all using fresh, local ingredients. Now, there is an endless variety of ingredients available all year, perfect for traditional one-pot cooking. Hot-pots are always cooked slowly for a long time, allowing the rich flavors to permeate the chicken.

Serves 4
4 chicken quarters
6 medium potatoes, cut into ¼-inch slices
2 sprigs thyme
2 sprigs rosemary
2 bay leaves
1 cup diced smoked bacon
1 large onion, finely chopped
1 cup sliced carrots
²/₃ cup dark beer or stout
2 tbsp melted butter
salt and pepper
seasonal vegetables, to serve

1 Remove the skin from the chicken quarters if desired.

2 Arrange a layer of potatoes in the bottom of a wide casserole. Season to taste with salt and pepper, then add the herbs.

3 Top with the chicken quarters, then sprinkle with the diced bacon, onion, and carrots. Season to taste, and arrange the remaining potatoes on top, overlapping slightly.

4 Pour in the beer or stout, brush the potatoes with the melted butter, and cover with a lid.

5 Bake in a preheated oven at 300°F for about 2 hours, uncovering for the last 30 minutes to allow the potatoes to brown. Serve hot, with fresh seasonal vegetables.

Country Chicken Bake

This economical bake is a complete meal to cook and serve in one pot—and it is easy to adjust for any amount of servings. Its crusty, herb-flavored French bread topping mops up the tasty juices, and means there is no need to serve potatoes or rice separately.

Serves 4
2 tbsp sunflower oil
4 chicken quarters
16 small whole onions, peeled
3 celery stalks, sliced
14 ounce can red kidney beans
4 medium tomatoes, quartered
scant 1 cup hard cider or stock
4 tbsp chopped fresh parsley
1 tsp paprika
4 tbsp butter
12 slices French bread
salt and pepper

1 Heat the oil in a flameproof casserole and fry the chicken quarters, two at a time, until golden all over. Remove from the casserole and set aside.

2 Add the onions and fry, turning occasionally, until golden brown. Add the celery and fry for 2–3 minutes.

3 Return the chicken to the pan and stir in the beans, tomatoes, cider, half the parsley, and salt and pepper. Sprinkle with the paprika. Cover and cook in a preheated oven at 400°F for 20–25 minutes, until the juices run clear when the chicken is pierced with the point of a sharp knife.

4 Mix the remaining parsley with the butter and spread evenly over the French bread.

5 Uncover the casserole, arrange the bread slices overlapping on top, and

bake for a further 10–12 minutes, until the topping is golden and crisp. Serve immediately.

Add a crushed garlic clove to the parsley butter for extra flavor.

Quick Chicken Dishes

One of the marvelous qualities of chicken is that when cut into small pieces, it can be cooked very quickly, which is welcome for those of us who are too busy to spend a lot of time preparing meals. In this section, you can select a tasty nutritious dish that willl not take hours to make. Pasta makes a perfect partner for chicken as it is also quick to cook. Look for Pasta Medley and Italian Chicken Spirals. Smaller cuts of chicken are also ideal for stir-fries that can be quickly cooked to produce tender, moist and flavorful chicken.

Speedy Peanut Pan-fry is a crunchy stir-fry that is served with noodles, while Chicken & Almond Rissoles with Stir-fried Vegetables offers chicken and potato rissoles with a nutty coating that are served with a colorful mixture of crunchy flash-cooked vegetables.

Chicken with Lemon & Tarragon

Chicken fillets are cooked with saffron, white wine, and stock flavored
with lemon rind and tarragon, then the sauce is thickened with
egg yolks and sour cream, and finished with mayonnaise.

Serves 6
6 large skinless, boneless chicken breasts
¹/₄ tsp saffron strands
1 cup boiling water
1 tbsp olive oil
2 tbsp butter
1 garlic clove, crushed
¹/₂ cup dry white wine
grated rind of 1 small lemon
1 tbsp lemon juice
1–2 tbsp chopped fresh tarragon
2 tsp cornstarch
1 egg yolk
6 tbsp sour cream or heavy cream
4 tbsp thick mayonnaise
salt and pepper

TO GARNISH

sprigs of fresh tarragon
lemon twists

1 Cut each chicken breast almost
horizontally into three thin slices
with a sharp knife. Season each piece
well with salt and pepper.

2 Put the saffron strands into a bowl,
pour on the boiling water, and let
stand until needed.

3 Heat the oil, butter, and garlic in a
heavy-based skillet. When foaming,
add the chicken and fry on each side
until lightly colored.

4 Add the saffron liquid, wine, lemon
rind and juice, and half the tarragon.
Bring to a boil, lower the heat, and
simmer for about 5 minutes, until the
chicken is tender.

5 Remove the chicken with a slotted
spoon and place on a serving dish in
overlapping slices. Set aside to cool.
Boil the remaining juices in the skillet
for 3–4 minutes to reduce slightly.

6 Blend the cornstarch, egg yolk, and
cream together in a bowl. Whisk in a
little of the cooking juices, then pour
the mixture into the skillet, and heat
gently, stirring continuously, until

thickened and just barely simmering.
Remove from the heat, adjust the
seasoning, and pour into a bowl.
Cover and set aside until cool.

7 Beat the mayonnaise and remaining
fresh tarragon into the sauce and
spoon it over the chicken. Cover and
chill thoroughly. Garnish with sprigs
of fresh tarragon and lemon twists.

Pasta Medley

Strips of cooked chicken are tossed with colored pasta, grapes, and carrot sticks in a pesto-flavoured dressing. Any leftovers can be kept in the refrigerator for a day or two.

Serves 2
4–5 ounces dried pasta shapes, such as twists or bows
1 tbsp oil
2 tbsp mayonnaise
2 tsp pesto sauce
1 tbsp sour cream or natural ricotta
6 oz cooked skinless, boneless chicken meat
1–2 celery stalks
1 cup black grapes (preferably seedless)
1 large carrot, trimmed
salt and pepper
celery leaves, to garnish

FRENCH DRESSING

1 tbsp wine vinegar
3 tbsp extra-virgin olive oil
salt and pepper

1 To make the French dressing, whisk all the ingredients together until thoroughly combined and smooth.

2 Cook the pasta with the oil in plenty of boiling, salted water for about 12 minutes, until just tender. Drain thoroughly, rinse, and drain again. Transfer to a bowl and mix in 1 tablespoon of the French dressing while hot. Set aside until cold.

3 Combine the mayonnaise, pesto sauce, and sour cream or ricotta in a bowl, and season to taste.

4 Cut the chicken into narrow strips. Cut the celery diagonally into narrow

slices. Reserve a few grapes for garnish, halve the rest, and remove any pips. Cut the carrot into narrow julienne strips.

5 Add the chicken, celery, halved grapes, carrot, and mayonnaise mixture to the pasta, and toss

thoroughly. Check the seasoning, adding more salt and pepper if necessary.

6 Arrange the pasta medley on two plates, garnish with the reserved black grapes and the celery leaves and serve at once.

Tagliatelle with Chicken & Almonds

Spinach tagliatelle with a rich tomato sauce and creamy
chicken makes a very appetizing dish.

Serves 4
¹/₄ cup sweet butter
14 ounces skinless, boneless chicken breasts, sliced thinly
³/₄ cup blanched almonds
1¹/₄ cups heavy cream
8 ounces fresh green ribbon noodles
salt and pepper
basil leaves, to garnish

TOMATO SAUCE

1 small onion, chopped
2 tbsp olive oil
1 garlic clove, chopped
14 ounce can chopped tomatoes
2 tbsp chopped fresh parsley
1 tsp dried oregano
2 bay leaves
2 tbsp tomato paste
1 tsp sugar

1 To make the tomato sauce, sauté the onion gently in the oil until translucent. Add the garlic and sauté for 1 further minute. Stir in the remaining ingredients and bring to a boil. Simmer, uncovered, for 15–20 minutes, until reduced by half. Discard the bay leaves and keep the sauce warm.

2 Melt the butter in a heavy-based skillet and fry the chicken and almonds gently, stirring frequently, for 5–6 minutes.

3 Meanwhile, boil the cream in a small pan for about 10 minutes, until reduced by almost half.

4 Stir the cream into the chicken mixture and season with salt and pepper. Set aside and keep warm.

5 Cook the pasta in a large pan of boiling salted water until just tender.

Drain the pasta and turn into a warm serving dish.

6 Spoon the tomato sauce over the pasta with the chicken mixture in the center. Garnish with basil and serve.

Tortellini

According to legend, tortellini are said
to resemble Venus's navel.

Serves 4
4 ounces cooked skinless, boneless chicken breasts, chopped
2 ounces prosciutto
1¹/₂ ounces cooked drained spinach
1 tbsp finely chopped onion
2 tbsp grated Parmesan
pinch of ground allspice
1 egg, beaten
salt and pepper

PASTA DOUGH

pinch of salt
generous 2¹/₂ cups flour
3 large eggs
1 tbsp olive oil
1 tbsp water

SAUCE

1¹/₄ cups light cream
1–2 garlic cloves, crushed
1¹/₂ cups mushrooms, thinly sliced
4 tbsp freshly grated Parmesan
1–2 tbsp chopped fresh parsley
salt and pepper

1 To make the pasta dough, sift the flour and salt onto a flat surface. Make a well in the center. Beat the eggs, oil, and water together, pour into the well and work together to form a dough. Knead for about 10–15 minutes. Cover with a damp cloth and set aside for 10–15 minutes.

2 Process the chicken with the Parma ham, spinach, and onion, in a food processor until finely chopped. Add the Parmesan cheese, allspice, seasoning, and egg.

3 Roll out the dough, half at a time, very thinly. Cut into 1½-inch rounds. Place ½ teaspoon of the filling on each. Fold into a semicircle and seal the edges. Wrap the semicircle around your finger, crossing the ends. Press together and curl the rest of the dough back. Place on a floured tray. Repeat with the rest of the dough.

4 Cook in batches. Once they rise to the surface, cook for 5 minutes. Drain, keep warm, and cook the remainder. For the sauce, heat the cream and garlic and bring to a boil. Add the mushrooms and half the Parmesan. Simmer for 2 minutes. Add the parsley and pour onto the pasta. Sprinkle with the remaining Parmesan and serve.

Chicken Kiev

This classic dish from the Ukraine is delicious
served with sautéed potatoes.

Serves 4
1 garlic clove, crushed
⅓ cup butter
4 skinless, boneless chicken breasts
oil for deep-frying
1 cup all-purpose flour
2 eggs, beaten
2 tbsp milk
bread crumbs, for coating
salt and pepper

TO GARNISH

chopped parsley
lemon wedges

1 Mash the garlic into the butter with a fork. Season well and shape into a square patty. Chill in the freezer while you prepare the chicken.

2 Slice each chicken breast horizontally in half, and lay between sheets of plastic wrap. Flatten each piece to an even thickness. Discard the plastic wrap.

3 When the butter is quite hard, cut it into four batons. Place a baton lengthwise on four of the chicken breast slices. Cover each with another chicken breast slice and refrigerate until ready to serve.

4 Beat the eggs and milk together. When ready to serve, add oil to a pan to a depth of about 2 inches and heat to a moderate, deep-frying temperature, about 375°F. Coat each Kiev with flour, then the egg mixture, and finally with bread crumbs. Repeat once to form a good seal. Fry each Kiev for about 5 minutes. Serve at once while still piping hot.

COOK'S TIP

About 1 tablespoon fresh chopped parsley can be added to the garlic and butter.

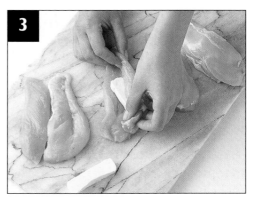

Chicken & Almond Rissoles with Stir-fried Vegetables

Cooked potatoes and cooked chicken are combined to make tasty rissoles, rolled in chopped almonds, then served with stir-fried vegetables.

Serves 1
4 ounces boiled potatoes
3 ounces carrots
1 cup cooked chicken meat
1 garlic clove, crushed
$\frac{1}{2}$ tsp dried tarragon or thyme
pinch of ground allspice or ground coriander seeds
1 egg yolk, or $\frac{1}{2}$ egg, beaten
about $\frac{1}{4}$ cup slivered almonds
salt and pepper

STIR-FRIED VEGETABLES

1 celery stalk
2 scallions, trimmed
1 tbsp oil
8 baby corn cobs
about 10–12 snow peas or sugar snap peas, trimmed
2 tsp balsamic vinegar
salt and pepper

1 Coarsely grate the boiled potatoes and raw carrots into a bowl. Chop finely or grind the chicken and add to the vegetables with the garlic, tarragon, allspice or coriander, and plenty of salt and pepper.

2 Add the egg yolk or beaten egg and bind the ingredients together. Divide in half and shape into 2 "sausages."

3 Finely chop the almonds and then roll each rissole in the nuts until evenly coated.

4 Place the rissoles in a greased ovenproof dish and cook in a preheated oven at 400°F for about

20 minutes or until lightly browned. Alternatively, fry in a little oil until browned all over and cooked through.

5 While the rissoles cook, prepare the stir-fried vegetables. Cut the celery and scallions diagonally into thin slices. Heat the oil in a skillet and toss in the vegetables. Stir-fry over high heat for 1–2 minutes, then add the corn cobs and peas, and cook for

2–3 minutes. Finally, add the balsamic vinegar and season with salt and pepper to taste.

6 Spoon the stir-fried vegetables onto a serving plate and place the rissoles beside them. Serve at once.

Chicken with Peanut Sauce

A tangy stir-fry with a strong peanut flavor.
Serve with freshly boiled rice or noodles.

Serves 4
4 skinless, boneless chicken breasts, weighing 1¼ pounds
4 tbsp soy sauce
4 tbsp sherry
3 tbsp crunchy peanut butter
12 ounces zucchini, trimmed
2 tbsp sunflower oil
4–6 scallions, thinly sliced diagonally
8 ounce can bamboo shoots, drained and sliced
salt and pepper
4 tbsp shredded coconut, toasted, to garnish

1 Cut the chicken into thin strips across the grain and season lightly with salt and pepper.

2 Put the soy sauce in a bowl, together with the sherry and peanut butter, and stir until smooth and thoroughly blended.

3 Cut the zucchini into 2-inch lengths and then cut into sticks about ¼-inch thick.

4 Heat the oil in a preheated wok, swirling it around until it is really hot. Add the scallions and stir-fry for a minute or so, until translucent. Then add the chicken and stir-fry for 3–4 minutes, until well sealed and almost cooked.

5 Add the zucchini and bamboo shoots and continue to stir-fry for 1–2 minutes.

6 Add the peanut butter mixture and heat thoroughly, stirring all the time so that everything is coated in the sauce as it thickens. Adjust the seasoning and serve very hot, sprinkled with the toasted coconut.

COOK'S TIP

If desired, smooth peanut butter can be used instead of the crunchy variety.

Chicken with Celery & Cashew Nuts

Yellow bean sauce, widely available bottled, gives this easy Chinese dish a really authentic taste. Pecan nuts can be used in place of the cashews.

Serves 4

3–4 skinless, boneless chicken
breasts, weighing 1¼ pounds

2 tbsp sunflower
or vegetable oil

1 cup unsalted cashew nuts

4–6 scallions, thinly
sliced diagonally

5–6 celery stalks, thinly
sliced diagonally

6 ounce jar yellow
bean sauce

salt and pepper

celery leaves, to
garnish (optional)

boiled rice,
to serve

1 Cut the chicken into thin slices across the grain.

2 Heat the oil in a preheated wok, swirling it around until really hot. Add the cashew nuts and stir-fry until they begin to brown, then add the chicken, and stir-fry until well sealed and almost cooked through.

3 Add the scallions and celery and continue to stir-fry for 2–3 minutes, keeping the ingredients moving around the wok.

4 Add the yellow bean sauce, season lightly with salt and pepper, and toss until the chicken and vegetables are thoroughly coated with the sauce and piping hot. Serve at once with plain boiled rice, garnished with celery leaves, if using.

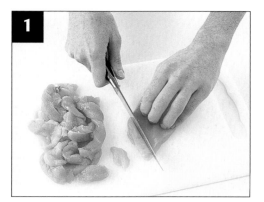

Pan-cooked Chicken with Artichokes

Artichokes are a familiar ingredient in Italian cookery.
In this dish, they are used as a delicate flavoring with chicken.

Serves 4
4 chicken breasts, part boned
2 tbsp olive oil
2 tbsp butter
2 red onions, cut into wedges
2 tbsp lemon juice
²/₃ cup dry white wine
²/₃ cup chicken stock
2 tsp all-purpose flour
14 ounce can artichoke hearts, drained and halved
salt and pepper
chopped fresh parsley, to garnish

1 Season the chicken to taste with salt and pepper. Heat the oil, together with1 tablespoon of the butter, in a large heavy-based skillet. Add the chicken and fry gently for 4–5 minutes on each side, until lightly golden. Remove from the skillet with a slotted spoon.

2 Toss the onions in the lemon juice, and add to the skillet. Sauté gently, stirring, for 3–4 minutes, until just beginning to soften.

3 Return the chicken to the skillet. Pour in the wine and stock, bring to a boil, then cover, and simmer gently for 30 minutes.

4 Remove the chicken from the skillet, reserving the cooking juices. Keep warm. Bring the juices to a boil, and boil rapidly for 5 minutes.

5 Blend the remaining butter with the flour to form a paste. Reduce the heat so that the pan juices are just simmering and add the paste to the skillet, a little at a time, stirring until the sauce has thickened.

6 Adjust the seasoning, stir in the artichoke hearts, and cook for a further 2 minutes. Pour the sauce over the chicken and garnish with parsley.

Poached Breast of Chicken with Whiskey Sauce

After cooking with stock and vegetables, chicken breasts are served with a velvety sauce made from whiskey and crème fraîche.

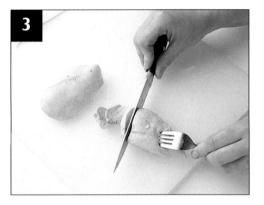

Serves 6
2 tbsp butter
$^{1}/_{2}$ cup shredded leeks
$^{1}/_{3}$ cup diced carrot
$^{1}/_{4}$ cup diced celery
4 shallots, sliced
2$^{1}/_{2}$ cups chicken stock
6 chicken breasts
$^{1}/_{4}$ cup whiskey
1 cup crème fraîche
2 tbsp freshly grated horseradish
1 tsp honey, warmed
1 tsp chopped fresh parsley
salt and pepper
parsley, to garnish

1 Melt the butter in a large saucepan and add the leeks, carrot, celery, and shallots. Cook for 3 minutes, add half the chicken stock, and cook for about 8 minutes.

2 Add the remaining chicken stock, bring to a boil, add the chicken breasts, and cook for 10 minutes.

3 Remove the chicken and thinly slice. Place on a large, warm serving dish and keep warm.

4 In another saucepan, heat the whiskey until reduced by half. Strain the chicken stock through a fine strainer, add to the pan, and reduce the liquid by half.

5 Add the crème fraîche, horseradish, and honey. Heat gently and stir in the parsley. Season with salt and pepper to taste.

6 Pour a little of the whiskey sauce around the chicken and pour the remaining sauce into a sauce boat to serve.

7 Serve with a vegetable patty made from the leftover vegetables, mashed potato, and fresh vegetables. Garnish with parsley.

Garlicky Chicken Cushions

Stuffed with creamy ricotta, spinach, and garlic, then gently cooked in
a rich tomato sauce, this is a suitable dish to make ahead of time.

Serves 4
4 part-boned chicken breasts
$^1/_2$ cup frozen spinach, thawed
$^1/_2$ cup ricotta cheese
2 garlic cloves, crushed
1 tbsp olive oil
1 onion, chopped
1 red bell pepper, seeded and sliced
14 ounce can chopped tomatoes
6 tbsp wine or chicken stock
10 stuffed olives, sliced
salt and pepper
flat leaf parsley sprigs, to garnish
pasta, to serve

5 Bring the sauce to a boil, pour it into a shallow ovenproof dish, and arrange the chicken breasts on top in a single layer.

6 Cook, uncovered, in a preheated oven at 400°F for 35 minutes until the chicken is golden and cooked through.

Test by making a slit in one of the chicken breasts with a sharp knife to make sure the juices run clear with no hint of pink. Spoon a little of the sauce over the chicken breasts, then transfer to warm serving plates, and garnish with parsley. Serve immediately with pasta.

1 Make a slit between the skin and meat on one side of each chicken breast. Lift the skin to form a pocket, being careful to leave the skin attached to the other side.

2 Put the spinach into a strainer and press out the water with a spoon. Mix with the ricotta and half the garlic and season to taste.

3 Spoon the spinach mixture evenly under the skin of each chicken breast, then secure the edge of the skin with toothpicks.

4 Heat the oil in a skillet, add the onion, and sauté, stirring, for a minute. Add the remaining garlic and the bell pepper and cook for 2 minutes. Stir in the tomatoes, wine or stock, olives, and seasoning. Set the sauce aside and chill the chicken if preparing in advance.

Mediterranean Chicken Packets

This method of cooking makes the chicken aromatic and succulent.

Serves 6
1 tbsp olive oil
6 skinless, chicken breast fillets
2 cups mozzarella cheese
3½ cups sliced zucchini
6 large tomatoes, sliced
1 small bunch fresh basil
or oregano
pepper
rice or pasta,
to serve

1 Cut six pieces of foil each about 10 inches square. Brush the foil squares lightly with oil.

2 With a sharp knife, slash each chicken breast at intervals, then slice the cheese, and place between the cuts in the chicken.

3 Divide the zucchini and tomatoes among the pieces of foil and sprinkle with black pepper. Tear or roughly chop the herbs and scatter them over the vegetables.

4 Place the chicken on top of each pile of vegetables, then wrap in the foil to enclose the chicken and vegetables, tucking in the ends.

5 Place on a cookie sheet and bake in a preheated oven at 400°F for about 30 minutes. To serve, unwrap each foil packet, and serve on warm plates with rice or pasta.

Steamed Chicken & Spring Vegetable Packets

A healthy recipe with a delicate Eastern flavor, ideal for tender young summer vegetables. You will need large spinach leaves to wrap around the chicken, but make sure they are young leaves.

Serves 4
4 boneless, skinless chicken breasts
1 tsp ground lemon grass
2 scallions, finely chopped
8 ounces young carrots
8 ounces young zucchini
2 celery stalks
1 tsp light soy sauce
8 ounces spinach leaves
2 tsp sesame oil
salt and pepper

1 With a sharp knife, make a slit through one side of each chicken breast to open out a large pocket. Sprinkle the inside of the pocket with lemon grass, salt, and pepper. Tuck the scallions into the chicken pockets.

2 Trim the carrots, zucchini, and celery, then cut into small matchsticks. Plunge them into a pan of boiling water for 1 minute, then drain, and toss in the soy sauce.

3 Pack into the pockets in each chicken breast and fold over firmly to enclose. Reserve the remaining vegetables. Wash and dry the spinach leaves, then wrap the chicken breasts firmly in the leaves to enclose them completely. If the leaves are too firm to wrap the chicken easily, steam them for a few seconds until they are softened and flexible.

4 Place the wrapped chicken in a steamer and steam over rapidly boiling water for 20–25 minutes, depending on size.

5 Stir-fry any leftover vegetable sticks and spinach in the sesame oil for 1–2 minutes and serve with the chicken packets.

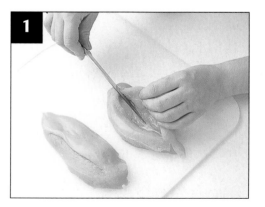

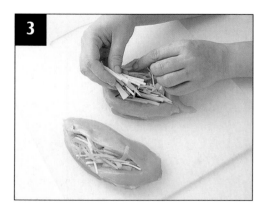

Prosciutto Wrapped Chicken Cushions

Stuffed with creamy ricotta, nutmeg, and spinach, then wrapped with wafer-thin
slices of prosciutto and gently cooked in white wine.

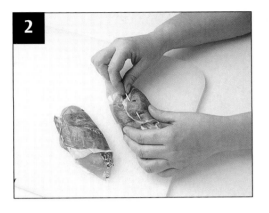

Serves 4
¹/₂ cup frozen spinach, thawed
¹/₂ cup ricotta cheese
pinch grated nutmeg
4 skinless, boneless chicken breasts, each weighing 6 ounces
4 slices prosciutto
2 tbsp butter
1 tbsp olive oil
12 small onions or shallots
1¹/₂ cups sliced button mushrooms
1 tbsp all-purpose flour
²/₃ cup dry white or red wine
1¹/₄ cups chicken stock
flat leaf parsley sprigs, to garnish
carrot purée and green beans, to serve

1 Put the spinach into a strainer and press out the water with the back of a spoon. Mix with the ricotta and nutmeg and season to taste with salt and pepper.

2 Slit each chicken breast through the side and enlarge each cut to form a pocket. Fill with the spinach mixture, reshape the chicken breasts, wrap each in a slice of prosciutto, and secure with toothpicks. Cover and chill in the refrigerator.

3 Heat the butter and oil in a heavy-based skillet and fry the chicken breasts for 2 minutes on each side. Transfer the chicken to a large, shallow ovenproof dish.

4 Fry the onions and mushrooms for 2–3 minutes until lightly browned.

Stir in the flour, then gradually add the wine and stock. Bring to a boil, stirring. Season to taste and spoon the mixture around the chicken.

5 Cook the chicken, uncovered, in a preheated oven at 400°F for

20 minutes. Turn the breasts over and cook for a further 10 minutes. Remove the toothpicks and serve with the sauce, garnished with the parsley. Serve with carrot purée and green beans, if desired.

Chicken Lady Jayne

If you prefer, just use boneless chicken breasts in this recipe.
This dish has a surprising combination of coffee and brandy flavors.

Serves 4
1 pound chicken breasts or suprêmes
4 tbsp corn oil
8 shallots, sliced
rind and juice of 1 lemon
2 tsp Worcestershire sauce
4 tbsp chicken stock
1 tbsp chopped fresh parsley
3 tbsp coffee liqueur
3 tbsp brandy, warmed

1 Cut the chicken breasts into 4 even pieces, cover them with plastic wrap, and beat them flat with a wooden meat mallet or a rolling pin.

2 Heat the oil in a large skillet and fry the chicken for 3 minutes on each side. Add the shallots and cook for a further 3 minutes.

3 Sprinkle with lemon juice and lemon rind and add the Worcestershire sauce and chicken stock. Cook for 2 minutes, then sprinkle with the parsley. Finally, add the coffee liqueur and the brandy and flame the chicken by lighting the spirit with a taper or long match. Cook until the flame is extinguished and serve immediately.

COOK'S TIP

A suprême is a chicken fillet that sometimes has part of the wing bone remaining. Chicken breasts can be used instead.

Chicken Risotto alla Milanese

This famous dish is known throughout the world, and it is perhaps the best known of all Italian risottos, although there are many variations.

Serves 4
$^1/_2$ cup butter
$1^3/_4$ pounds chicken meat, thinly sliced
1 large onion, chopped
$2^1/_2$ cups risotto rice
$2^1/_2$ cups chicken stock
$^2/_3$ cup white wine
1 tsp crumbled saffron
salt and pepper
$^1/_2$ cup grated Parmesan cheese, to serve

1 Melt 4 tbsp of butter in a deep skillet, add the chicken and onion, and cook, stirring frequently, until golden brown.

2 Add the rice, stir well, and cook, stirring constantly, for 5 minutes.

3 Heat the stock until boiling and add to the rice. Add the white wine, saffron, salt, and pepper and mix well. Simmer gently for 20 minutes, stirring occasionally.

4 Let stand for a few minutes and just before serving add a little more stock, and simmer for a further 10 minutes. Serve, sprinkled with the cheese and the remaining butter.

COOK'S TIP

There are many types of risotto rice with short, round grains. Arborio is a typical Italian risotto rice that is found in most supermarkets.

Savory Chicken Sausages

Served with a smooth, creamy tomato sauce,
this makes an excellent light lunch with freshly baked cheese bread.

Serves 4–6
3 cups fresh bread crumbs
8 ounces cooked chicken, ground
1 small leek, finely chopped
pinch each of mixed herbs and mustard powder
2 eggs, separated
4 tbsp milk
crisp bread crumbs for coating
2 tbsp beef drippings
salt and pepper
tomato sauce, to serve

1 In a large bowl, mix together the bread crumbs, chicken, leek, herbs, and mustard powder and season with salt and pepper.

2 Add 1 whole egg and an egg yolk with a little milk to bind the mixture.

3 Divide the mixture into 6 or 8 and shape into thick or thin sausages.

4 Whisk the remaining egg white until frothy. Coat the sausages first in the egg white and then in the crisp bread crumbs.

5 Heat the drippings and fry the sausages for 6 minutes until golden brown. Serve the sausages with a little tomato sauce.

COOK'S VARIATION

If you want to lower saturated fat in this recipe, use a little oil for frying instead of the drippings.

Tom's Toad-in-the-Hole

This unusual recipe uses chicken and Cumberland sausage,
which is then made into individual bite-size cakes.

Serves 4–6
1 cup all-purpose flour
pinch of salt
1 egg, beaten
1 scant cup milk
$^1/_3$ cup water
8 ounces chicken breasts
8 ounces Cumberland sausage
2 tbsp beef drippings
chicken or onion gravy, to serve (optional)

1 Mix the flour and salt in a bowl, make a well in the center, and add the beaten egg.

2 Add half the milk, and using a wooden spoon, gradually work in the flour.

3 Beat the mixture until it is smooth and free of lumps, then stir in the remaining milk and water.

4 Beat again until the mixture is smooth. Let the mixture stand for at least 1 hour. Add the drippings to individual muffin pans or to one large roasting pan.

5 Cut up the chicken and sausage so that there will be a generous portion in each individual pan or several scattered around the large pan.

6 Heat the pans in a preheated oven at 425°F for 5 minutes, until very hot. Remove the pans from the oven and pour in the batter, leaving space for the mixture to expand.

7 Return to the oven to cook for 35 minutes, until risen and golden brown. Do not open the oven door for at least 30 minutes.

8 Serve while hot, with chicken or onion gravy, or alone.

COOK'S VARIATION

Use skinless, boneless chicken legs instead of chicken breast in the recipe. Cut up as directed. Instead of Cumberland sausage, use your favorite variety of sausage.

Deviled Chicken

Chicken is spiked with cayenne and paprika and finished off with a fruity sauce.

Serves 2–3
¼ cup all-purpose flour
1 tbsp cayenne pepper, plus extra for sprinkling
1 tsp paprika
12 ounces skinless, boneless chicken, diced
2 tbsp butter
1 onion, finely chopped
2 cups milk, warmed
4 tbsp apple purée
¾ cup white grapes
⅔ cup sour cream

1 Mix the flour, cayenne, and paprika together and use to coat the chicken all over.

2 Shake off any excess flour. Melt the butter in a saucepan and gently fry the chicken with the onion for 4 minutes.

3 Stir in the flour and spice mixture and gradually blend in the milk, stirring until the sauce thickens.

4 Simmer until the sauce is smooth.

5 Add the apple purée and grapes and simmer gently for 20 minutes.

6 Transfer the chicken and deviled sauce to a warm serving dish and top with sour cream and a sprinkling of paprika.

Quick Chicken Bake

This recipe is a type of cottage pie and is just as versatile. Add vegetables and herbs of your choice, depending on what you have at hand.

Serves 4
1 pound ground chicken
1 large onion, finely chopped
2 carrots, finely diced
2 tbsp all-purpose flour
1 tbsp tomato paste
1^1/$_4$ cups chicken stock
pinch of fresh thyme
1^3/$_4$ pounds potatoes, creamed with butter and milk and highly seasoned
^{3}/$_4$ cup grated Lancashire cheese or other semihard, white cheese
salt and pepper
peas, to serve

1 Dry-fry the minced chicken, onion, and carrots in a nonstick saucepan for 5 minutes.

2 Sprinkle the chicken with the flour and simmer for a further 2 minutes.

3 Gradually blend in the tomato paste and stock, then simmer for 15 minutes. Season with salt and pepper to taste and add the thyme.

4 Transfer the chicken mixture to a casserole and allow to cool.

5 Top the chicken with the mashed potato and sprinkle with the cheese. Bake in a preheated oven at 400°F for 20 minutes, then serve with peas.

Chicken in Rum & Orange Cream Sauce

A rich, orange cream sauce that is simplicity itself. Its luxurious texture comes from crème fraîche, but you can use light cream instead.

Serves 4
2 tbsp sunflower oil
8 small, skinless chicken drumsticks
3 shallots or scallions, finely chopped
1 cup orange juice
4 tbsp dark rum
1 cup long-grain rice
grated rind of $1/2$ orange
1 cup crème fraîche or light cream
salt and pepper
orange segments (optional) and parsley, to garnish

1 Heat the oil in a large skillet, add the chicken and onions, and fry over moderate heat until browned all over.

2 Add the orange juice and rum, cover tightly, and simmer for about 15 minutes, or until the juices run clear when the thickest part of the chicken is pierced with the point of a sharp knife.

3 Meanwhile, cook the rice in boiling, lightly salted water until just tender. Drain and stir in the orange rind.

4 Stir the crème fraîche into the chicken and bring to a boil.

5 Season to taste with salt and pepper. Serve the chicken with the orange rice, garnished with orange segments, if using, and parsley.

Speedy Peanut Pan-fry

A complete main course cooked within ten minutes. Thread egg noodles are the ideal accompaniment because they can be cooked quickly and easily while the stir-fry sizzles, but any type of pasta or rice can be served instead.

Serves 4
2 cups zucchini
1¹/₃ cups baby corn cobs
3 cups thread egg noodles
2 tbsp corn oil
1 tbsp sesame oil
8 boneless chicken thighs
or 4 chicken breasts, thinly sliced
3³/₄ cups button mushrooms
1¹/₂ cups bean sprouts
4 tbsp smooth peanut butter
2 tbsp soy sauce
2 tbsp lime or lemon juice
¹/₂ cup roasted peanuts
salt and pepper
sprigs of fresh cilantro,
to garnish

COOK'S TIP

Try serving this stir–fry with rice sticks. These are broad, pale, translucent ribbon noodles made from ground rice.

1 Trim and thinly slice the zucchini and corn cobs.

2 Cook the noodles in lightly salted boiling water for 3–4 minutes. Meanwhile, heat the corn oil and sesame oil in a large skillet or wok and fry the chicken over fairly high heat for 1 minute.

3 Add the zucchini, corn, and mushrooms and stir-fry for 5 minutes.

4 Add the bean sprouts, peanut butter, soy sauce, lime juice, and pepper, then cook for a further 2 minutes.

5 Drain the noodles. Scatter with the peanuts, garnish with cilantro, and serve with the noodles.

Italian Chicken Spirals

Steaming allows you to cook without fat, and these little foil packets retain all the natural juices of the chicken while cooking conveniently over the pasta while it boils. Sun-dried tomatoes, preserved in oil, have a wonderful, rich flavor, but if you cannot find them, use fresh tomatoes.

Serves 4
4 skinless, boneless chicken breasts
1 cup fresh basil leaves
2 tbsp hazelnuts
1 garlic clove, crushed
2 cups whole-wheat pasta spirals
2 sun-dried tomatoes
or fresh tomatoes
1 tbsp lemon juice
1 tbsp olive oil
1 tbsp capers
$\frac{1}{2}$ cup black olives
salt and pepper
sprigs of fresh basil, to garnish
tomato salad, to serve

1 Beat the chicken breasts with a rolling pin to flatten evenly.

2 Place the basil and hazelnuts in a food processor and process until finely chopped. Mix with the garlic, salt, and pepper.

3 Spread the basil mixture over the chicken breasts and roll up from one short end to enclose the filling. Wrap the chicken rolls tightly in foil so that they hold their shape, then seal the ends well.

4 Add the pasta to a large pan of lightly salted, boiling water. Place the chicken packets in a steamer basket or colander set over the pan, cover tightly, and steam for 10 minutes. Meanwhile, dice the tomatoes.

5 Drain the pasta and return to the pan with the lemon juice, olive oil,

tomatoes, capers, and olives. Heat until warmed through.

6 Pierce the chicken with the point of a sharp knife to make sure that the

juices run clear and not pink, then slice the chicken, and arrange over the pasta on a warm serving dish. Garnish with sprigs of basil and serve with a tomato salad.

Golden Glazed Chicken

A glossy glaze with sweet and fruity flavors coats chicken breasts in this tasty recipe.

Serves 6
6 boneless chicken breasts
1 tsp turmeric
1 tbsp whole-grain mustard
1¼ cups orange juice
2 tbsp clear honey
2 tbsp sunflower oil
1½ cups long-grain rice
1 orange
3 tbsp chopped mint
salt and pepper
mint sprigs, to garnish

1 With a sharp knife, mark the surface of the chicken breasts in a diamond pattern. Mix together the turmeric, mustard, orange juice, and honey and pour over the chicken. Set aside to marinate in the refrigerator until required.

2 Lift the chicken from the marinade and pat dry on paper towels. Reserve the marinade.

3 Heat the oil in a wide pan, add the chicken, and sauté until golden, turning once. Drain off any excess oil. Pour the marinade into the pan, cover, and simmer for 10–15 minutes, until the chicken is tender.

4 Boil the rice in lightly salted water until tender, and drain well. Finely grate the rind from the orange and stir into the rice with the mint.

5 Remove the peel and white pith from the orange and segment.

6 Serve the chicken with the orange and mint rice, garnished with orange segments and mint sprigs.

COOK'S VARIATION

To make a slightly sharper sauce, use small grapefruit instead of the oranges.

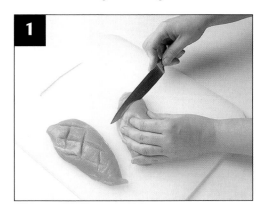

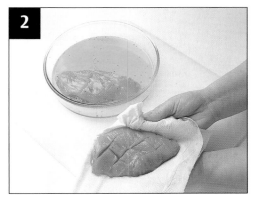

Harlequin Chicken

This colorful, simple dish will tempt the appetites of all the family—it is ideal for young children, who enjoy the fun shapes of the multicolored bell peppers.

Serves 4
10 skinless, boneless chicken thighs
1 medium onion
1 medium red bell pepper
1 medium green bell pepper
1 medium yellow bell pepper
1 tbsp sunflower oil
14 ounce can chopped tomatoes
2 tbsp chopped fresh parsley
pepper
whole-wheat bread and salad greens, to serve

1 Cut the chicken thighs into bite-size pieces.

2 Peel and thinly slice the onion. Seed the bell peppers and cut the flesh into small diamond shapes.

3 Heat the oil in a shallow skillet, then quickly fry the chicken and onion until golden.

4 Add the bell peppers, cook for 2–3 minutes, stir in the tomatoes and parsley, and season with pepper.

5 Cover tightly and simmer for about 15 minutes, until the chicken and vegetables are tender. Serve hot with whole-wheat bread and salad greens.

COOK'S TIP

If you are making this dish for small children, the chicken can be finely chopped or ground first.

Golden Chicken Risotto

If you prefer, ordinary long-grain rice can be used instead of risotto rice, but it will not give you the traditional, deliciously creamy texture that is typical of Italian risottos.

Serves 4
2tbsp sunflower oil
1 tbsp butter or margarine
1 medium leek, thinly sliced
1 large yellow bell pepper, seeded and diced
3 skinless, boneless chicken breasts, diced
2 cups risotto rice
few strands saffron
6 1/4 cups chicken stock
7 ounce can corn cobs
1/2 cup toasted unsalted peanuts
1/2 cup grated Parmesan cheese
salt and pepper
salad greens, to serve

1 Heat the oil and butter in a large skillet. Fry the leek and bell pepper for 1 minute, then stir in the chicken, and cook, stirring until golden brown.

2 Stir in the rice and cook for 2–3 minutes.

3 Add the saffron, chicken stock, salt, and pepper. Cover and cook over low heat, stirring occasionally, for about 20 minutes, until the rice is tender and most of the liquid has been absorbed. Add more stock or water if necessary.

4 Stir in the corn cobs, peanuts, and Parmesan cheese, then adjust the seasoning to taste.

5 Serve hot with crisp salad greens.

Elizabethan Chicken

Chicken is surprisingly delicious when combined
with fruit, such as grapes or gooseberries.

Serves 4
1 tbsp butter
1 tbsp sunflower oil
4 skinless, boneless chicken breasts
4 shallots, finely chopped
$^2/_3$ cup chicken stock
1 tbsp cider vinegar
1 cup halved seedless grapes
$^1/_2$ cup heavy cream
1 tsp freshly grated nutmeg
cornstarch, to thicken, (optional)
salt and pepper

1 Heat the butter and oil in a wide,
flameproof casserole or pan and
quickly fry the chicken breasts until
golden brown, turning once. Remove
and keep hot.

2 Add the shallots to the pan and
sauté gently until softened and lightly
browned. Return the chicken breasts
to the pan.

3 Add the stock and vinegar, bring
to a boil, then cover, and simmer
gently, stirring occasionally, for
10–12 minutes.

4 Transfer the chicken to a warm
serving dish. Add the grapes, cream,
and nutmeg to the pan. Heat through,
season to taste, and thicken with a
little cornstarch if desired. Serve the
chicken with the hot sauce.

Chicken, Corn, & Snow Pea Sauté

This quick and healthy dish is stir-fried, which means you need use only the minimum of fat. If you do not have a wok, use a wide skillet instead.

Serves 4
4 skinless, boneless chicken breasts
1$^1/_3$ cups baby corn cobs
8 ounces snow peas
2 tbsp sunflower oil
1 tbsp sherry vinegar
1 tbsp honey
1 tbsp light soy sauce
1 tbsp sunflower seeds
pepper
rice or Chinese egg noodles, to serve

1 With a sharp knife, slice the chicken breasts into long, thin strips. Cut the corn cobs in half lengthwise and top and tail the snow peas.

2 Heat the oil in a wok or a wide skillet and fry the chicken over fairly high heat, stirring, for 1 minute.

3 Add the corn and snow peas and stir over moderate heat for about 5–8 minutes, until evenly cooked.

4 Mix together the sherry vinegar, honey, and soy sauce and stir into the wok or skillet with the sunflower seeds. Season well with pepper. Cook, stirring, for 1 minute. Serve hot with rice or Chinese egg noodles.

COOK'S TIP

Rice vinegar or balsamic vinegar makes a good substitute for the sherry vinegar.

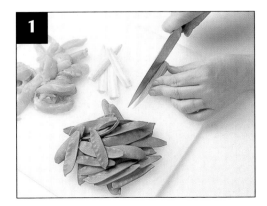

Chicken Strips & Dips

Very simple to make and easy to eat with fingers, this dish can be served warm for a light lunch or cold as part of a buffet. For a lower fat alternative, poach the strips of chicken in a small amount of boiling chicken stock for 6–8 minutes, or until thoroughly cooked.

Serves 2
2 boneless chicken breasts
2 tbsp all-purpose flour
1 tbsp sunflower oil
vegetable sticks, to serve

PEANUT DIP
3 tbsp smooth or crunchy peanut butter
4 tbsp unsweetened yogurt
1 tsp grated orange rind
orange juice (optional)

TOMATO DIP
5 tbsp creamy ricotta
1 medium tomato, finely chopped
2 tsp tomato paste
1 tsp chopped fresh chives

1 Slice the chicken into fairly thin strips and toss in the flour to coat.

2 Heat the oil in a nonstick skillet and fry the chicken until golden and thoroughly cooked. Drain well on absorbent paper towels.

3 To make the peanut dip, mix together all the ingredients (if desired, add a little orange juice to thin the consistency).

4 Combine the ingredients for the tomato dip and mix well.

5 Serve the chicken strips with the dips and a selection of vegetable sticks for dipping.

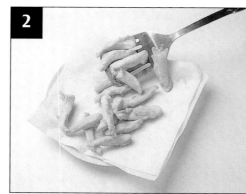

Chicken with Two Bell Pepper Sauce

This quick and simple dish is colorful and healthy. It would be perfect for an impromptu lunch or supper dish.

Serves 4
2 tbsp olive oil
2 medium onions, finely chopped
2 garlic cloves, crushed
2 red bell peppers, seeded and chopped
pinch of cayenne pepper
2 tsp tomato paste
2 yellow bell peppers, seeded and chopped
pinch of dried basil
4 skinless, boneless chicken breasts
$2/3$ cup dry white wine
$2/3$ cup chicken stock
bouquet garni
salt and pepper
fresh herbs, to garnish

4 Put the chicken breasts into a skillet and add the wine and stock. Add the bouquet garni and bring the liquid to simmering point. Cook the chicken for about 20 minutes, until tender.

5 To serve, put a pool of each sauce onto four serving plates, slice the chicken breasts, and arrange on the plates. Garnish with fresh herbs and serve immediately.

1 Heat 1 tablespoon of oil in each of two medium saucepans. Place half the chopped onions, 1 of the garlic cloves, the red bell peppers, the cayenne pepper, and the tomato paste in one of the saucepans. Place the remaining onion and garlic, the yellow bell peppers, and basil in the other pan.

2 Cover each pan and cook over a very low heat for 1 hour, until the bell peppers are very soft. If either mixture becomes dry, add a little water. Process the contents of each pan separately in a food processor, then press each through a strainer with the back of a spoon.

3 Return to the pans and season to taste with salt and pepper. The two sauces can be gently re-heated while the chicken is cooking.

Pies, Pastries, & Terrines

Chicken once again shows its versatility in a splendid array of pastries and pies. Many of the pies and terrines can be made ahead of time and served cold, making them a good choice for a buffet, picnic, or lunch. A thin slice of a terrine or pie can be served as a starter or a light meal, while a hearty slice of a traditional pie, such as Raised Chicken Pie, served with pickles and salad, makes a satisfying main course. Various pastries are used for the pies, a choux pastry topping adorns Chicken

and Corn Puff, while Sesame Chicken Pies, Chicken Filo Packets, and Stilton & Walnut Strudel are all made from sheets of filo pastry. A suet pastry is used to make Old-Fashioned Chicken Pudding, and for Chicken, Cheese, & Tarragon Pie, the base is made from pie dough while the topping is a golden puff pastry.

Chicken & Corn Puff

This delicious choux puff is an impressive dish yet it is simple to make.
You can use the choux pastry as a topping for all kinds of filling.

Serves 4
2 tbsp butter or margarine
$1/4$ cup all-purpose flour
$1^{1/4}$ cups skim milk
1 cup skinless, boneless cooked chicken, shredded
$3/4$ cup canned corn cobs, drained
1 tbsp chopped fresh parsley
salt and pepper

CHOUX PASTRY

generous $1/2$ cup all-purpose flour
$1/4$ cup butter or margarine
$2/3$ cup water
2 eggs, beaten
salt

1 To make the choux pastry, sift the flour and salt into a bowl. Put the butter or margarine and water into a large pan, then heat gently until the butter has melted. Bring to a boil. Remove from the heat and add the flour all at once. Beat with a wooden spoon until the mixture comes away from the sides of the pan cleanly. Set aside to cool slightly.

2 Gradually beat in the eggs until the mixture is thick and very glossy.

3 To make the filling, put the butter or margarine, flour, and milk into a saucepan. Heat, whisking constantly, until smooth and thickened.

4 Add the chicken, corn, and parsley to the sauce. Season to taste with salt and pepper. Pour into a 4-cup shallow ovenproof dish.

5 Spoon the choux pastry around the edge of the dish. Bake in a preheated oven at 425°F for 35–40 minutes, until puffed up and golden brown. Serve at once.

Three Fillet Packet

Fillets of chicken, lamb, and pork are layered with sage leaves, wrapped in spinach leaves, covered with a layer of cottage cheese, and enclosed in puff pastry. This is delicious served cold and cut into slices.

Serves 6
10–12 ounces pork fillet or tenderloin
about 12 fresh sage leaves
8–10 ounces lamb neck fillet
2 skinless, boneless chicken breasts, weighing 10 ounces
2 tbsp oil
4 ounces large spinach leaves
12 ounces puff pastry, thawed if frozen
1 cup cottage cheese
pinch of ground allspice
pinch of garlic powder
beaten egg or milk to glaze
salt and pepper
TO GARNISH
sage leaves
cucumber slices

1 Layer the fillets, beginning with the pork fillet. Cover with half the sage leaves, then add the lamb fillet, the rest of the sage leaves, and finally the chicken fillets. Secure with string.

2 Heat the oil in a skillet and fry the layered fillets for about 15 minutes, turning until browned and partly cooked. Remove from the skillet and set aside until cold.

3 Blanch the spinach leaves in boiling water for 2 minutes and drain well.

4 Thinly roll out the pastry into a rectangle large enough to enclose the layered fillets and allow for five narrow strips to be cut off the edge.

Cut off the strips, then lay the spinach in the center of the pastry. Spread with the cottage cheese. Season to taste with salt and pepper and add the allspice and garlic powder.

5 Remove the string and place the fillets on top of the cheese and spinach. Wrap up in the pastry and

seal the edges. Place on a greased cookie sheet and glaze with egg. Lay strips of pastry over the roll and glaze.

6 Bake in a preheated oven at 400°F for 30 minutes. Reduce the temperature to 350°F and bake for 20 minutes. Cool, then chill. Slice and garnish with sage and cucumber.

Raised Chicken Pie

A filling of diced chicken leg meat, ground pork, and bacon with pickled
walnuts, mushrooms, and herbs is enclosed in a hot-water pastry crust.

Serves 6
12 ounces skinless, boneless chicken thighs
$1/2$ cup lean pork, ground
$1/2$ cup coarsely ground or finely chopped cooked ham
1 small onion, very finely chopped
$2/3$ cup button mushrooms, roughly chopped
1 tbsp chopped fresh parsley
pinch of ground coriander seeds
6 pickled walnuts, drained
beaten egg or milk to glaze
1 tsp powdered gelatin
$2/3$ cup chicken stock
salt and pepper

PASTRY
3 cups all-purpose flour
1 tsp salt
$1/3$ cup shortening
6 tbsp water
3 tbsp milk, for glazing

1 To make the filling, chop the
chicken thighs and mix with the pork,
ham, onion, mushrooms, parsley, and
ground coriander. Season to taste
with salt and pepper.

2 To make the pastry, sift the flour
and salt into a bowl. Melt the
shortening in a saucepan with the
water and milk and then bring to a
boil. Pour onto the flour and mix to
an even dough.

3 Roll out about three-quarters of the
dough and use to line a lightly
greased raised pie mold or a loaf pan.

4 Add half the chicken mixture to the
mold, then a layer of walnuts, and the
remaining chicken. Roll out the
reserved pastry, position over the
chicken as a lid and cut a hole in the
center. Add pastry leaves and glaze.

5 Bake on a cookie sheet in a
preheated oven at 400°F for

30 minutes. Reduce the temperature
to 350°F, glaze, and bake for 1 hour.
Remove from the oven. Cool for
10 minutes.

6 Dissolve the gelatin in the stock.
Add as much stock as possible through
the lid. Cool, then chill for 12 hours.
Unmold before serving.

Chicken & Ham Pie

Made with yogurt pie dough, this pie has a really
moist filling and a melt-in-your-mouth crust.

Serves 6
¹/₄ cup butter
¹/₄ cup all-purpose flour
²/₃ cup milk
²/₃ cup unsweetened yogurt
2 small leeks, sliced
8 ounces skinless, boneless chicken breasts, diced
1¹/₃ cups ham, diced
1 tsp soy sauce
black pepper
dill sprigs, to garnish

PIE DOUGH

2 cups all-purpose flour, plus extra for dusting
¹/₂ tsp mustard powder
¹/₄ tsp salt
³/₄ cup butter, diced
about 3 tbsp natural yogurt
2 tbsp milk to glaze

1 To make the pie dough, grease a
loose-based flan pan, 1¾ inches deep.
Sift together the flour, mustard
powder, and salt. Rub in the butter
until the mixture resembles fine
bread crumbs. Stir in just enough
yogurt to make a firm, non-sticky
dough. Wrap in foil and chill.

2 Melt 2 tablespoons of the butter in
a pan. Blend in the flour. Add the
milk and yogurt, stirring constantly.
Simmer, uncovered, for 5 minutes,
then transfer the sauce to a bowl, and
set aside to cool.

3 Melt the remaining butter in a pan
and sauté the leeks for 2–3 minutes.

4 Pour the sauce over the leeks, add
the chicken and ham, and cook for
3 minutes. Add the soy sauce, season
with pepper, then let cool.

5 Roll out the dough on a floured
board. Use just over half to line the
prepared pan. Add the filling. Roll out
the remaining dough and cover the
pie. Trim the edges and press together.
Brush the top with milk to glaze. Re-
roll the trimmings and cut into
decorative shapes. Arrange over the
pie and brush with milk. Bake in a
preheated oven at 400°F for
35 minutes, or until golden.

Sussex Huffed Pie

This modern version of a very old English classic uses chicken breasts wrapped in a light and crisp crust of vegetable suet crust pastry. The apple and walnut stuffing adds a delicious moist filling to each little packet.

Serves 4
3 cups self-rising flour, sifted
1¼ cups vegetable suet
4 skinless, boneless chicken breasts
1 small cooking apple, thinly sliced
¼ cup chopped walnuts
2 tbsp chopped fresh sage
2 tbsp Worcestershire sauce
milk, to glaze
salt and pepper

1 Mix the flour and suet, and season with salt and pepper. Stir in just enough cold water to bind to a firm, but not sticky dough. Divide into 4 and roll out each piece of dough to an 8-inch round.

2 Cut a slit in the side of each chicken breast and pack with apple slices, walnuts, and sage. Brush the pastry rounds all over with Worcestershire sauce.

3 Place a chicken breast on each pastry round.

4 Fold the pastry over and pinch the edges of the pastry together to seal. Lift onto a cookie sheet and glaze with milk. Bake in a preheated oven at 400°F for 30–35 minutes, until golden brown. Serve hot or cold.

Nell Gwynn's Chicken Pie

A traditional old English type of pie, subtly flavored with oranges. If you prefer, it can be made with chicken off the bone instead of cuts.

Serves 4
8 skinless chicken cuts (drumsticks and thighs)
$^1\!/_2$ cup baby onions
1 large orange
$^1\!/_2$ cup chicken stock
8 ounces chilled or frozen puff pastry, thawed
milk, for brushing
salt and pepper
green vegetables, to serve
FORCEMEAT
$1^1\!/_2$ cups fresh whole-wheat bread crumbs
2 tbsp finely chopped cooked ham
2 tbsp chopped fresh parsley
finely grated rind 1 orange
1 tbsp sunflower oil
1 egg, beaten

1 Mix together all the ingredients for the forcemeat and season well with salt and pepper. Shape the mixture into 8 small balls.

2 Fry the chicken joints in a nonstick skillet without fat, turning occasionally, until golden brown. Drain well on paper towels and transfer to a $7^1\!/_2$-cup pie dish.

3 Plunge the onions into a pan of boiling water and boil for 1 minute. Drain, rinse in cold water, and remove the skins.

4 With a sharp knife, cut away all the peel and white pith from the orange, then remove the segments. Add the onions, orange, and forcemeat balls to the dish. Add the stock and season to taste with salt and pepper.

5 Roll out the pastry slightly larger than the pie dish and cut a 1-inch wide strip from the edge. Brush the rim of the dish with milk and press on the strip of pastry to fit.

6 Cover the pie with the large piece of pastry. Press the edges to seal and brush with the milk. Place on a cookie sheet in a preheated oven at 425°F for 10 minutes. Reduce the heat to 325°F and bake for a further hour. Serve hot with fresh green vegetables.

Chicken, Stilton, & Walnut Strudel

A perfect choice for a cold buffet table, or serve hot with a red wine gravy for a dinner party main course. The combination of Stilton, mushrooms, and walnuts helps enrich and moisten the filling without the need for a sauce to bind the ingredients. The strudel slices more easily when cold.

Serves 5–6
4 tbsp butter
2 cups oyster or flat mushrooms, sliced
2 shallots or scallions, finely chopped
1 pound boneless, cooked chicken thighs, finely chopped
¹/₂ cup walnut pieces
1¹/₃ cups crumbled Stilton cheese
3 tbsp ricotta cheese
1 tbsp chopped fresh thyme
7 sheets of filo pastry, each measuring 7¹/₂ x14 inches
pepper
salad or vegetables, to serve

1 Melt 2 tablespoons of the butter and sauté the mushrooms, shallots, and chicken until the shallots are softened and translucent and any free liquid has evaporated.

2 Reserve a few walnuts for the garnish and combine the rest with the mushrooms, shallots, chicken, Stilton cheese, ricotta, and thyme. Season with pepper.

3 Melt the remaining butter. Brush each sheet of pastry with butter, then overlap the sheets to make one large square. Spoon the chicken mixture into the center of the square.

4 Roll up carefully to enclose the filling, tucking in the ends.

5 Lift the roll carefully onto a greased cookie sheet, brush with butter, and scatter with the remaining walnuts. Bake in a preheated oven at 375°F for 25–30 minutes, until golden brown and firm. Serve hot or cold, with salad or vegetables.

COOK'S TIP

Ricotta is an Italian whey cheese with a creamy, bland flavor and a soft, smooth texture. It should be used within 24 hours of purchase.

Chicken Filo Packets

Perfect for a picnic, these tasty chicken packets can
be packed into a rigid plastic container for carrying.

Serves 6
$1/2$ cup frozen spinach, thawed
$1/2$ cup feta cheese
6 skinless, boneless chicken thighs
12 sheets filo pastry, each measuring $7^{1}/_{2}$ x14 inches
2 tbsp sunflower oil
1 tbsp poppy seeds
pepper
tomato salad, to serve

1 Place the spinach in a strainer and press out excess moisture. Crumble the cheese, then mix with the spinach, and season with pepper.

2 Open out the chicken thighs on a board and place a spoonful of the spinach mixture on each. Fold over the chicken to enclose the filling.

3 Lightly brush the sheets of filo pastry with oil. Sandwich together in pairs, then place a piece of chicken on each. Roll up the pastry, tucking in the ends to enclose the filling.

4 Place on a cookie sheet and brush with oil, then sprinkle with poppy seeds. Bake in a preheated oven at 400°F for 30–35 minutes, until golden brown and bubbling. Cool on a wire rack. Serve with a tomato salad.

Sesame Chicken Pies

This chicken pie is easy to make with ready-made filo pastry. Thigh meat is very economical and you can buy it ready diced, or just buy boneless thighs and chop them at home.

Serves 4
1 pound diced chicken thigh meat
1 tbsp cornstarch
1 cup crème fraîche
1 tbsp chopped fresh chives
1 medium onion, thinly sliced
$1/2$ cup chicken stock
11 ounce can corn cobs, drained
4 sheets filo pastry
2 tbsp olive oil
1 tsp sesame seeds
salt and pepper
green vegetables, to serve

6 Bake a large pie in a preheated oven at 375°F for 50–60 minutes, or individual pies for 30–35 minutes, until golden brown. Serve hot with green vegetables.

COOK'S TIP

Packaged filo pastry is available fresh and frozen. It can be stored for up to 1 year in the freezer.

1 Toss the chicken in the cornstarch to coat evenly. Stir in the crème fraîche and chives and season to taste with salt and pepper.

2 Place the onion in a pan with the chicken stock and simmer over a moderate heat, stirring, until the onion is softened and most of the stock has evaporated. Add the corn to the chicken.

3 Transfer the mixture to a large pie dish or divide among four 1¼-cup ovenproof dishes. Place on a cookie sheet.

4 Spread out the filo pastry and brush with oil.

5 Scrunch up the pastry to cover the filling of each pie. Sprinkle with sesame seeds.

Chicken wrapped in Puff Pastry with Lancashire Cheese & Mustard

This recipe is a variation on the classic Beef Wellington—and just as delicious.

Serves 6–8
1 pound chicken breast meat
3 tbsp butter
2 onions, finely chopped
1¹/₂ cups button mushrooms or exotic mushrooms
2 ready-rolled sheets puff pastry
2 tbsp English mustard
4 ounces chicken liver pâté
³/₄ cup crumbled Lancashire cheese or other semihard white cheese
1 egg, lightly beaten
salt and pepper

1 With a sharp knife, trim the fat from the chicken and season well with salt and pepper.

2 Melt 2 tablespoons of the butter in a large, heavy-based skillet, add the chicken, and cook for about 4 minutes until sealed.

3 Add the remaining butter to the skillet and add the chopped onion and mushrooms. Cook until all the moisture has evaporated, then set aside to cool.

4 Roll out half the pastry to a large rectangle and place on a greased cookie sheet.

5 Spread the onion and mushroom mixture in the center of the pastry and place the chicken on top.

6 Top the chicken breasts with the mustard and liver pâté, then sprinkle them with a layer of the crumbled white cheese

7 Roll out the remaining pastry so it is slightly larger than the base.

8 Brush the edges of the pastry with egg then press together to seal.

9 Slash the top of the pastry with a sharp knife, then brush with egg.

10 Bake in the center of a preheated oven at 400°F for 20 minutes, then lower the oven temperature to 350°F for a further 20 minutes, until the pie is golden brown.

Roast Chicken & Cranberry Pie

Cranberries are a good accompaniment to poultry
and make this pie very tasty, whether served hot or cold.

Serves 6
4 tbsp butter
2 leeks, finely sliced
8 shallots, sliced
1½ cups sliced mushrooms
¼ cup all-purpose flour
1¼ cups milk, warmed
⅔ cup heavy cream
1 pound roast chicken meat, diced
1 cup cranberry sauce
6 ounces pie dough, thawed if frozen
4 ounces puff pastry, thawed if frozen
1 egg, beaten, for glazing
salt and pepper

1 Melt the butter in a large saucepan, add the leeks, shallots, and mushrooms, and gently sauté, stirring occasionally, for about 10 minutes.

2 Add the flour and cook, stirring, for a further 2 minutes.

3 Gradually add the warm milk and cream, stirring continuously until the sauce becomes thick and creamy. Simmer for 2 minutes.

4 Add the chicken and cranberry sauce to the mixture.

5 Season well with salt and pepper and set the mixture aside to cool.

6 Roll out the pie dough for the base and use to line a greased ovenproof pie dish. Add the chicken mixture and top with the puff pastry. Brush the top of the pie with the beaten egg. Bake in the center of a preheated oven at 400°F for 30 minutes until risen and golden brown.

COOK'S TIP

Dried cranberries would make an interesting addition to the pie instead of the ready-made cranberry sauce.

Chicken, Cheese, & Tarragon Pie

The best way to prepare this type of pie is to make
a pie dough base with a puff pastry topping.

Serves 6
4 tbsp butter
2 carrots, finely diced
8 shallots, sliced
3 cups button mushrooms, sliced
1/4 cup all-purpose flour
1 1/4 cups milk, warmed
2/3 cup heavy cream
1 pound chicken breast, cooked and diced
3 tbsp chopped fresh tarragon
1/2 cup grated Cheddar cheese
6 ounces pie dough, thawed if frozen
4 ounces puff pastry, thawed if frozen
1 egg, for glazing
salt and pepper
garlic creamed potatoes and green vegetable or salad, to serve

1 Melt the butter in a large saucepan, add the carrots, shallots, and button mushrooms, and gently sauté, stirring occasionally, for about 10 minutes.

2 Add the flour and cook, stirring, for a further 2 minutes.

3 Gradually add the milk and cream, stirring continuously until the sauce becomes thick and creamy.

4 Simmer, stirring from time to time, for 2 minutes.

5 Add the cooked chicken breast, tarragon, and cheese to the sauce.

6 Season well with salt and pepper and set the mixture aside to cool.

7 Roll out the pie dough base and use to line a greased, oval ovenproof pie dish.

8 Add the chicken mixture and top with puff pastry. Brush with the beaten egg to glaze and bake in the center of a preheated oven at 400°F for 30 minutes, or until the top is risen and golden.

9 Serve immediately with garlic creamed potatoes and a green vegetable or salad.

Old-Fashioned Chicken Pudding

This is a recipe from yesteryear made with suet pastry. Vegetable suet, which is made from hydrogenated vegetable oil, is now an option if you do not want to use suet made from animal fat.

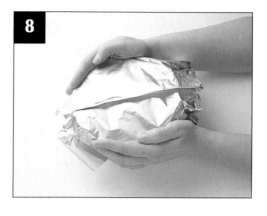

Serves 4
4 tbsp butter
pinch of fines herbes
4 skinless chicken breasts, sliced
1¼ cups button mushrooms
4 shallots, sliced
²⁄₃ cup fresh orange juice
1 sprig fresh thyme
4 tbsp brandy
²⁄₃ cup game or chicken stock, thickened
8 ounces suet pastry
salt and pepper
fresh vegetables, to serve

1 Melt the butter in a large skillet, add the fines herbes, sliced chicken breasts, button mushrooms, and shallots and pan-fry them for 6 minutes. Remove the breasts from the skillet.

2 Add the orange juice, thyme, brandy, and seasoning to the skillet and simmer for at least 20 minutes, until the liquid is reduced by half.

3 Add the game or chicken stock, simmer, and again reduce by half.

4 Line an 8-inch heatproof bowl with suet pastry.

5 Put the meat and game or chicken stock into the bowl.

6 Cover the top of the bowl with suet pastry and press the pastry layers gently together to seal.

7 Brush the top with melted butter.

8 Cover the bowl with several layers of cooking foil.

9 Steam the pudding in a covered saucepan for 2 hours, topping up the pan with extra water as necessary. Serve with fresh vegetables.

COOK'S TIP

Fines herbes is a classic mixture of parsley, chervil, tarragon, and chives that is often used in French cooking.

Springtime Creamed Chicken & Vegetable Quiche

A quick-and-easy quiche that can be made even speedier
if you use ready-made pie dough.

Serves 4–6
12 ounces pie dough, thawed if frozen
2 tbsp butter
6 scallions
1 cup shredded leeks, (white parts only)
1½ cups button mushrooms
1 cup peas
1¼ cups grated Cheddar cheese
6 ounces cooked chicken meat, thinly sliced
3 eggs
1 egg yolk
⅔ cup each milk and heavy cream, mixed
salt and pepper

1 Roll out the pie dough and use to line a 10-inch loose-based flan pan.

2 Melt the butter in a large skillet and sauté the scallions, leeks, mushrooms, and peas over low heat for 6 minutes.

3 Remove from the heat, sprinkle the base of the quiche with half the grated cheese, then add the chicken and vegetables.

4 Top with the remaining cheese.

5 Beat the eggs, egg yolk, and the milk and cream mixture together and pour it over the chicken and vegetables in the pastry shell.

6 Bake in the center of a preheated oven at 375°F for 35–45 minutes, until the filling is set and golden brown. Serve hot or cold.

COOK'S VARIATION

If desired, substitute light cream for the milk and cream mixture.

1

4

5

Savory Criss Cross

This is a very tasty picnic bake which can be served hot or cold.
Try serving it with home-made ginger beer.

Serves 6
12 ounces ready-made pie dough
3 large hard-cooked eggs, sliced
8 slices lean, bacon, broiled and chopped
8 ounces cooked chicken, diced
1 1/2 cups sausage meat
1 egg beaten with 2/3 cup milk
salt and pepper

1 Roll out two thirds of the pie dough and use to line a buttered pie dish or a deep plate.

2 Arrange the eggs, bacon, chicken, and sausage meat in the pastry shell.

3 Pour the egg and milk mixture over the eggs and meat.

4 Season to taste with salt and pepper. Roll out the remaining pie dough and cut into thin strips about 1/2 inch wide, and lay them across the pie in a criss-cross pattern. Seal well all around the edges.

5 Bake in the center of a preheated oven at 400°F for 10 minutes. Reduce the oven temperature to 350°, and bake for a further 25 minutes. Serve hot or cold.

COOK'S TIP

Use your favorite sausages in this recipe—simply remove and discard the sausage skins, then loosen the sausage meat with a fork.

Terrine of Chicken & Ham with Cranberry & Shallot Marmalade

This is a very impressive terrine that would be suitable for any special occasion. The cranberry and shallot marmalade is a perfect accompaniment.

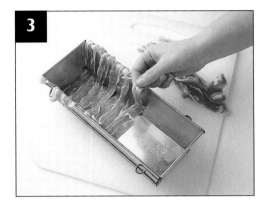

Serves 6–8
1 pound chicken meat, roughly chopped
$^1/_2$ cup sherry
$1^1/_2$ cups ground pork
1 small onion, chopped
3 eggs, beaten
1 pound lean cooked ham, diced
1 pound bacon
salt and pepper
orange slices, to garnish
crusty bread, to serve

CRANBERRY & SHALLOT MARMALADE

2 onions, chopped
2 tbsp butter
4 tbsp cranberries
1 tbsp brown sugar
8 shallots, chopped

1 Remove any fat or sinews from the chicken meat, place it in a bowl with the sherry, and marinate for 3 hours. Add the pork, onion, and the eggs. Season to taste with salt and pepper and mix thoroughly.

2 Stir the pieces of ham into the chicken mixture.

3 Line a 5-cup ovenproof terrine dish with the bacon slices.

4 Add the chicken mixture, top with the remaining bacon, then cover with greased cooking foil.

5 Bake in the center of a preheated oven at 350°F for 1½ hours. Remove the foil and set aside to cool naturally,

then chill in the refrigerator for at least 4 hours before serving.

6 For the cranberry and shallot marmalade, sauté the onions gently for 2 minutes in the butter. Season.

7 Add the cranberries, sugar, and shallots and cook for 5 minutes. Pour some of the marmalade onto individual plates beside a slice of the terrine. Garnish with orange slices and serve with fresh bread.

Terrine of Chicken & Black Pudding

This is a recipe that you can make ahead of time
and store chilled until needed.

Serves 6–8
1 pound boneless chicken meat, roughly chopped
1¹/₂ cups brandy
1¹/₂ cups ground pork
¹/₂ onion, chopped
rind of 1 orange
3 eggs, beaten
1 pound black pudding, diced
1 pound bacon
2 tbsp butter
salt and pepper
orange slices and parsley, to garnish

1 Remove any fat or skin from the chicken, place the meat in a bowl with the brandy, and marinate for 3 hours.

2 Add the pork, onion, orange rind, and beaten eggs. Season to taste with salt and pepper and stir the mixture thoroughly to combine.

3 Carefully add the black pudding to the mixture, without breaking it up.

4 Line a 5-cup ovenproof terrine dish with slices of bacon. Spoon in the chicken mixture, cover with the remaining bacon, then with greased cooking foil.

5 Stand the terrine in a baking pan and add sufficient hot water to come to halfway up the side of the terrine.

6 Bake in the center of a preheated oven at 350°F for 1¹/₂ hours. Remove

the foil and set aside to cool, then chill for at least 4 hours before serving. Serve the terrine cut into thick slices, garnished with orange slices and parsley.

COOK'S TIP

Look for black pudding that is low in fat.

Potted Chicken & Cheese Terrine

Make this terrine at least two weeks before using it. This allows all the wonderful flavors of the cheeses, chicken, spices, and sherry to blend together and mellow. Serve with warm oat cakes and a good port.

Serves 4
4 ounces Wensleydale cheese or other creamy white cheese
4 ounces Lancashire cheese or other semihard white cheese
12 ounces cooked chicken fillet, shredded
$1/2$ cup butter
1 tbsp English mustard
$2/3$ cup cream sherry
pinch of mace
pinch of cayenne pepper
1 cup butter

1 Crumble or grate the cheeses and place all the ingredients, except the butter, into a blender or food processor. Process to mix thoroughly, while slowly adding the sherry.

2 Place into individual ramekins and make the clarified butter.

3 Place the butter in a small saucepan and heat very gently, skimming off the foam as the butter heats.

4 Stand for 5 minutes, then strain the butter through cheesecloth.

5 Pour the clarified butter over the mixture in the ramekins, let cool, then chill in the refrigerator.

COOK'S TIP

Because the milk solids are not present in clarified butter, it keeps better than ordinary, unheated butter.

Chicken, Basil, & Walnut Terrine

A terrine is a chunky pâté, which takes its name from the deep rectangular dish in which it is baked. If you do not have a terrine, a loaf pan can be used instead. This moist, basil-flavored dish is ideal for summer meals and picnics, served with a simple salad.

Serves 6
8 ounces bacon
1½ pounds skinless, boneless chicken thighs
1 cup cream cheese or ricotta
¼ cup fresh basil leaves
1 tbsp sunflower oil
1 small onion, finely chopped
1 tbsp butter
7 ounces chicken livers, chopped
1 cup chopped mushrooms
½ cup chopped walnuts
salt and pepper
sautéed mushrooms, to garnish
salad and French bread, to serve

1 Stretch the bacon with the back of a knife and use to line a 7½-cup terrine dish or loaf pan.

2 Place one third of the chicken, the cream cheese, and the basil in a food processor and process until almost smooth. Season to taste with salt and pepper.

3 Heat the oil and sauté the onion gently to soften. Finely chop the rest of the chicken and add to the pan, stirring until lightly colored, but not browned. Remove from the heat, stir in the cheese mixture, and season.

4 Spoon half the mixture into the terrine dish, smoothing the top.

5 Melt the butter and fry the chicken livers and mushrooms, stirring, for 3–4 minutes, until the chicken livers are lightly colored.

6 Add the walnuts and spoon evenly over the chicken mixture. Top with the remaining chicken mixture.

7 Cover with a lid or foil and bake in a preheated oven at 350°F for 1–1¼ hours, or until there is no trace of pink juices. Remove from the oven and place a weight on top. Leave to cool completely before turning out, or serve straight from the terrine dish. Garnish with sautéed mushrooms and serve in slices, with salad and French bread.

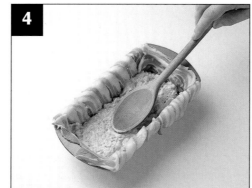

Chicken & Mushroom Terrine

This terrine is extremely quick to make if you use a food processor.
Sunflower seeds add a pleasing crunchy texture.

Serves 4
1 tbsp oil
1 pound skinless, boneless chicken breasts, roughly chopped
3 cups mushrooms
1 medium onion, quartered
1 garlic clove, crushed
$^1/_2$ cup fresh brown bread crumbs
3 tbsp chopped fresh parsley
3 tbsp chopped fresh sage
2 tbsp sunflower seeds
salt and pepper
crusty bread, to serve

1 Brush a 4-cup terrine dish or loaf pan with half the oil.

2 Place the chicken, mushrooms, and onion in a food processor and process until finely chopped.

3 Add the garlic, brown bread crumbs, parsley, sage, and sunflower seeds, then season to taste with salt and pepper.

4 Spoon the chicken mixture into the terrine and press down.

5 Brush with the remaining oil and loosely cover with foil. Bake in a preheated oven at 350°F for about 50 minutes, or until the juices run clear when the terrine is pierced with a toothpick. Cool in the terrine, then serve in thick slices with crusty bread.

Barbecues & Broils

There is nothing more delicious than the juicy flesh and charred skin of chicken that has been broiled over an open fire—after marinating in a flavorful mixture of oil and herbs or spices. Try an Asian-style mixture of yogurt and aromatic spices, or soy sauce, sesame oil, and fresh ginger root, or a Cajun-inspired marinade of warm spices and garlic for Blackened Chicken with Guacamole. In this section, chicken comes in all shapes and sizes, it is ground to make Lemon & Mint Chicken Burgers, butterflied for Barbecued Chicken, and cut into tiny, bite-size pieces for Spicy Chicken Tikka. There are some unusual flavors and innovative tastes, including Skewered Chicken with Bramble Sauce, and Skewered Chicken Spirals, which are attractive whirls of chicken, bacon, and basil. Rock Cornish hens, flavored with lemon and tarragon in this section, are perfect for broiling or barbecuing.

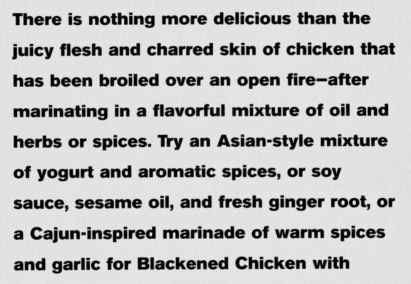

Lemon & Mint Chicken Burgers

Use chicken leg meat for these delicious burgers—it has
much more flavor than breast meat.

Serves 4
1¹/₂ pounds ground chicken leg meat
4 tbsp chopped fresh mint
grated rind of 1 lemon
juice of 1 lemon
olive oil
²/₃ cup pitted black olives, chopped
1 round focaccia bread, either plain or flavored
lettuce leaf and lemon slices, to garnish
salt
lemon pepper (or black pepper)

1 In a large bowl, combine the chicken, mint, lemon rind, lemon juice, 1 tablespoon of olive oil, black olives, salt, and lemon pepper. Set aside to marinate for at least 2 hours.

2 Form the mixture into four patties, eliminating any air holes by pressing between your hands. Return to the refrigerator until ready to serve.

3 When ready to serve, cut the focaccia into quarters, halve, and brush each piece with olive oil, and toast under a broiler—do not use a toaster.

4 Fry the chicken patties in a little olive oil, for about 10 minutes, until cooked through. Remove the patties with a slotted spoon and drain on paper towels. Put each patty between two pieces of bread, and serve, garnished with lettuce and lemon.

Barbecued Chicken

You need a bit of brute force to prepare the chicken, but once marinated it is an easy and tasty candidate for the barbecue. Take great care not to touch your eyes or lips while preparing the chili, and wash your hands thoroughly after handling.

Serves 4
3 pounds chicken
grated rind of 1 lemon
4 tbsp lemon juice
2 sprigs of rosemary
1 small red chili, seeded and finely chopped
$^2/_3$ cup olive oil
TO SERVE
minted new potatoes
salad greens

1 Split the chicken down the breast bone and open it out.

2 Break the leg and wing joints to enable you to pound it flat. This ensures that it cooks evenly.

3 Mix the lemon rind and juice, rosemary sprigs, chili, and olive oil together in a small bowl. Place the chicken in a large dish and pour the marinade over it, turning the chicken to coat it evenly. Cover the dish and marinate the chicken for at least 2 hours or overnight.

4 Cook the chicken over a hot barbecue for about 30 minutes, turning it regularly until the skin is golden and crisp. To test if it is cooked, pierce one of the chicken thighs with the point of a sharp knife; if it is ready, the juices should run clear, not pink. Serve with minted new potatoes and salad greens.

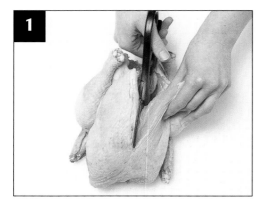

Chicken in Spicy Yogurt

Make sure the barbecue is really hot before you start cooking.
The coals should be white and glow red when fanned. You could also cook
the chicken under a very hot preheated broiler.

Serves 6
3 dried red chilies
2 tbsp coriander seeds
2 tsp turmeric
2 tsp garam masala
4 garlic cloves, crushed
$1/2$ onion, chopped
1-inch piece fresh ginger root, grated
2 tbsp lime juice
1 tsp salt
$1/2$ cup unsweetened yogurt
1 tbsp oil
4 pounds chicken, cut into 6 pieces or portions
TO SERVE
chopped tomatoes
diced cucumber
sliced red onion
cucumber and yogurt

1 Grind together the chilies, coriander seeds, turmeric, garam masala, garlic, onion, ginger, lime juice, and salt in a mortar with a pestle or in a grinder.

2 Heat a skillet over low heat and add the spice paste. Dry-fry, stirring, for about 2 minutes, until fragrant. Turn the spice paste into a shallow nonporous dish.

3 Add the yogurt to the spice paste and oil, and mix well to combine.

4 Remove the skin from the chicken portions and make three slashes in the flesh of each piece. Add the chicken to the dish and make sure

that the pieces are coated completely in the marinade. Cover and chill for at least 4 hours. Remove the dish from the refrigerator and leave covered at room temperature for 30 minutes before cooking.

5 Wrap the chicken pieces in foil, sealing well so the juices cannot

escape. Cook the chicken pieces over a very hot barbecue for about 15 minutes, turning once.

6 Remove the foil with tongs, and brown the chicken on the barbecue for 5 minutes. Serve with the chopped tomatoes, diced cucumber, sliced red onion, and yogurt mixture.

Charbroiled Chicken Salad

This is a quick dish to serve at a barbecue while your hungry guests are waiting for the main event. If the bread is bent in half, the chicken salad can be put in the middle and eaten as finger food—remember to provide napkins!

Serves 4
2 skinless, boneless chicken breasts
1 red onion
oil for brushing
1 avocado, peeled and pitted
1 tbsp lemon juice
$\frac{1}{2}$ cup mayonnaise
$\frac{1}{4}$ tsp chili powder
$\frac{1}{2}$ tsp pepper
$\frac{1}{4}$ tsp salt
4 tomatoes, quartered
$\frac{1}{2}$ loaf sun-dried tomato-flavored focaccia bread
salad greens, to serve

1 Cut the chicken breasts into $\frac{1}{2}$-inch strips.

2 Cut the onion into eight pieces, held together at the root. Rinse under cold running water and then brush with oil.

3 Purée or mash the avocado and lemon juice together. Whisk in the mayonnaise. Add the chili powder, pepper, and salt.

4 Put the chicken and onion over a hot barbecue and broil for 3–4 minutes on each side.

5 Combine the chicken, onion, tomatoes, and avocado mixture.

6 Cut the bread in half twice, so that you have quarter-circle-shaped pieces,

then in half horizontally. Toast on the hot barbecue for about 2 minutes on each side.

7 Spoon the chicken mixture on top of the toasts and serve at once with salad greens.

Mediterranean Broiled Chicken

Charbroiling and barbecuing are popular methods of cooking on the Mediterranean.
This recipe uses ingredients found in the Languedoc area of France,
where cooking over hot embers is a way of life.

Serves 4
4 tbsp unsweetened yogurt
3 tbsp sun-dried tomato paste
1 tbsp olive oil
$1/4$ cup fresh basil leaves, lightly crushed
2 garlic cloves, roughly chopped
4 chicken quarters
salad greens, to serve

1 Combine the yogurt, tomato paste, olive oil, basil leaves, and garlic in a small bowl and mix well.

2 Put the marinade into a bowl large enough to hold the chicken quarters in a single layer. Add the chicken quarters, making sure they are thoroughly coated in the marinade.

3 Marinate the chicken in the refrigerator for at least 2 hours or overnight. Remove and leave, covered, at room temperature for 30 minutes before cooking.

4 Place the chicken over a medium-hot barbecue and cook for 30–40 minutes, turning frequently.

5 Test for readiness by piercing the flesh at the thickest part—usually at the top of the drumstick. If the juices run clear, it is cooked through, but if the juices are pink, cook for 5–10 minutes longer.

6 Serve hot with salad greens. This dish is also delicious eaten cold.

Spicy Chicken Tikka

Arrange these tasty kabobs on a bed of finely shredded crisp lettuce, sliced onion, and grated apple, drizzled with a little lemon or lime juice.

Serves 6
1 pound skinless, boneless chicken breasts
1¹/₂ tbsp tikka paste (from a jar)
6 tbsp thick unsweetened yogurt
1 tbsp lemon juice
¹/₂ onion, finely chopped
1¹/₂ tbsp chopped fresh chives or scallion tops
1¹/₂ tbsp finely chopped fresh ginger root
1–2 garlic cloves, crushed
1¹/₂ tbsp sesame seeds
2 tbsp vegetable oil
salt and pepper
wedges of lemon or lime, to garnish

1 Cut the chicken breasts into small bite-size pieces, place in a shallow glass dish, and season with salt and pepper to taste.

2 In a small bowl, mix together the remaining ingredients, except the sesame seeds and oil, and pour over the chicken. Mix well until all the chicken pieces are completely coated, then cover with plastic wrap, and refrigerate for at least 1 hour, or for longer if possible.

3 Thread the chicken pieces onto six bamboo or metal skewers and sprinkle with the sesame seeds.

4 Place on a rack in a broiler pan and drizzle with the oil. Cook under a hot broiler for about 15 minutes or until cooked through and browned, turning frequently and brushing with more oil, if necessary. Serve hot, garnished with wedges of lemon or lime.

COOK'S TIP

Don't place the kabobs too near to the heat or the sesame seeds will burn before the chicken is cooked.

Tandoori Chicken

The tandoor is a traditional Indian oven shaped like a huge urn.
Charcoal is burnt slowly at the bottom until it becomes a mass of white-hot coals.

Serves 4
8 small skinless chicken portions
3 dried red chilies
1 tsp salt
2 tsp coriander seeds
2 tbsp lime juice
2 garlic cloves, crushed
1-inch piece fresh ginger root, grated
1 clove
2 tsp garam masala
2 tsp chili powder
1/2 onion, chopped
1 1/4 cups unsweetened yogurt
1 tbsp chopped fresh cilantro
lemon slices, to garnish

CUCUMBER RAITA

1 cup unsweetened yogurt
2 tsp chopped fresh mint
6 ounces cucumber, peeled, seeded, and cut into matchstick strips
salt

1 Make 2–3 slashes in the flesh of the chicken pieces and place in a nonmetallic dish.

2 Crush together the chilies, salt, coriander seeds, lime juice, garlic, ginger, and clove in a mortar with a pestle or process in a food processor. Stir in the garam masala and chili powder. Transfer to a small skillet and heat over low heat until aromatic.

3 Add the onion to the skillet and cook over low heat. Stir in the yogurt and remove the skillet from the heat.

4 Pour the yogurt mixture over the chicken. Cover and marinate in the refrigerator for 4 hours or overnight.

5 Combine the raita ingredients in a small bowl. Cover with plastic wrap and chill in the refrigerator.

6 Arrange the chicken on a broiler tray and cook under a preheated broiler or over a barbecue for 20–30 minutes, turning once, until the chicken juices run clear when the thickest parts of the portions are pierced with a sharp knife.

7 Sprinkle the chicken with chopped fresh cilantro. Serve hot or cold, garnished with the lemon slices and accompanied by the cucumber raita.

Sesame Skewered Chicken with Ginger Baste

Chunks of chicken breast are marinated in a mixture of lime juice, garlic, sesame oil, and fresh ginger to give them a spicy, aromatic flavor.

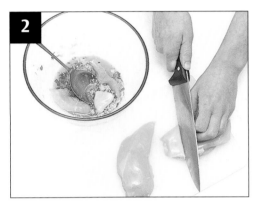

4 Place the kabobs under a preheated broiler for about 8–10 minutes. Turn them frequently, basting with the remaining marinade.

5 Serve at once, garnished with sprigs of fresh mint.

Serves 4
1 pound boneless chicken breasts
sprigs of fresh mint, to garnish
MARINADE
1 garlic clove, crushed
1 shallot, very finely chopped
2 tbsp sesame oil
1 tbsp fish sauce or light soy sauce
finely grated rind of 1 lime or $\frac{1}{2}$ lemon
2 tbsp lime juice or lemon juice
1 tsp sesame seeds
2 tsp finely grated fresh ginger root
2 tsp chopped fresh mint
salt and pepper

1 To make the marinade, put the garlic, shallot, sesame oil, fish sauce or soy sauce, lime or lemon rind and juice, sesame seeds, ginger, and chopped mint into a large nonmetallic bowl. Season to taste with a little salt and pepper.

2 Remove the skin from the chicken breasts and cut the flesh into chunks. Add them to the marinade, stirring to coat them in the mixture. Cover and chill for at least 2 hours. Soak four wooden satay sticks in warm water for 30 minutes

3 Thread the chicken onto the wooden satay sticks. Place them on the rack of a broiler pan and baste with the marinade.

Crispy Chicken Drumsticks

Just the thing to put on the barbecue—chicken drumsticks, coated with a spicy, curry-like butter, then broiled until crispy and golden. Serve with crisp seasonal salad greens and rice.

Serves 6
12 chicken drumsticks
SPICED BUTTER
³/₄ cup butter
2 garlic cloves, crushed
1 tsp grated fresh ginger root
2 tsp ground turmeric
4 tsp cayenne pepper
2 tbsp lime juice
3 tbsp mango chutney
TO SERVE
salad greens
boiled rice

5 Serve hot or cold with crisp salad greens and rice.

COOK'S TIP

Add a few drops of chili sauce to the spiced butter mixture to make the mixture hotter.

1 Prepare a barbecue with medium coals or preheat a broiler.

2 To make the spiced butter mixture, beat the butter with the garlic, ginger, turmeric, cayenne pepper, lime juice, and chutney until it is blended well.

3 Using a sharp knife, slash each chicken drumsticks to the bone 3–4 times. Cook them on a barbecue for about 12–15 minutes, or until almost cooked. Alternatively, broil the chicken for about 10–12 minutes, until almost cooked, turning once halfway through.

4 Spread the chicken drumsticks with the spicy butter mixture and continue to cook for a further 5–6 minutes, turning and basting frequently with the butter, until they are golden and crisp.

Blackened Chicken with Guacamole

This easy recipe is typical of French Cajun cooking which has its roots in earthy, strong flavors, and uses plenty of spice—a true classic.

Serves 4

4 skinless, boneless
chicken breasts

¼ cup butter, melted

SPICE MIX

1 tsp salt

1 tbsp sweet paprika

1 tsp dried onion granules

1 tsp dried garlic granules

1 tsp dried thyme

1 tsp cayenne

½ tsp cracked black pepper

½ tsp dried oregano

GUACAMOLE

1 avocado

1 tbsp lemon juice

2 tbsp sour cream

½ red onion, chopped

1 garlic clove, halved

1 Put each chicken breast between two pieces of plastic wrap, and pound with a mallet or rolling pin until it is an even thickness. It should be about ½ inch thick.

2 Brush each chicken breast all over with the melted butter. Set aside.

3 Combine the spice mix ingredients in a shallow bowl.

4 Coat the chicken breasts with the spice mix, ensuring that they are covered completely. Set aside.

5 To make the guacamole, put the avocado and the lemon in a small bowl and mash together thoroughly. Stir in the sour cream and red onion.

6 Rub the cut sides of the garlic clove all around the guacamole serving dish, pressing hard. Spoon in the guacamole.

7 Place the chicken breasts over the hottest part of a very hot barbecue and cook for 8–10 minutes, turning once.

8 Slice the breasts into thick pieces and serve immediately, handing the guacamole separately.

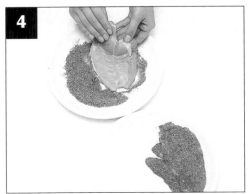

Jerk Chicken

This is a popular Caribbean dish. Rubbing pastes and "rubs" into meat, poultry, fish, or seafood is an old method of cooking introduced by the Arawak Indians that helps to tenderize the meat.

Serves 6
3 pounds chicken pieces
cherry tomatoes, to garnish
salad, to serve
MARINADE
6 scallions
2 fresh red chilies, preferably Scotch bonnet
2 tbsp dark soy sauce
2 tbsp lime juice
3 tsp ground allspice
$\frac{1}{2}$ tsp ground bay leaves
1 tsp ground cinnamon
2 garlic cloves, chopped
2 tsp brown sugar
1 tsp dried thyme
$\frac{1}{2}$ tsp salt

1 To make the marinade, chop the scallions. Seed and finely chop the chiles. Put the scallions, chilies, soy sauce, lime juice, allspice, ground bay leaves, cinnamon, garlic, sugar, thyme, and salt in a food processor or blender and process until smooth. Alternatively, finely chop the scallions and chilies (being careful not to touch your eyes), add these to the remaining ingredients and, using a pestle and mortar, pound to make a fairly chunky paste.

2 Place the chicken pieces in a shallow dish and spoon over the marinade, turning to coat thoroughly. Cover with plastic wrap and marinate in the refrigerator for 24 hours, turning each piece of chicken several times in the marinade.

3 Brush a broiler rack with oil and place the chicken on it. Broil under a preheated broiler for about 15–20 minutes on each side, until the chicken juices run clear when the thickest part of each piece is pierced with a sharp knife.

4 Garnish with cherry tomatoes and serve with a salad.

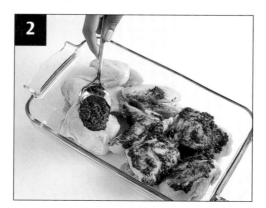

Filipino Chicken

This recipe is from the Philippines. Tomato ketchup is a very popular ingredient in Asian dishes, as it has a tangy, sweet-sour flavor.

Serves 4
1 can lemonade or lime-and-lemonade
2 tbsp gin
4 tbsp tomato ketchup
2 tsp garlic salt
2 tsp Worcestershire sauce
4 chicken suprêmes or breast fillets
salt and pepper

TO SERVE

thread egg noodles
1 green chili, finely chopped
2 scallions, sliced

1 Combine the lemonade or lime-and-lemonade, gin, tomato ketchup, garlic salt, Worcestershire sauce, and salt and pepper to taste in a large nonporous dish.

2 Put the chicken suprêmes into the dish. Cover the chicken completely with the marinade, turning it to coat all over.

3 Marinate in the refrigerator for 2 hours. Remove and leave, covered, at room temperature for 30 minutes.

4 Place the chicken over a medium barbecue and cook for 20 minutes, until cooked and tender. Turn the chicken once, halfway through the cooking time.

5 Remove from the barbecue and let rest for 3–4 minutes before serving.

6 Serve the chicken with egg noodles, tossed with a little green chili and sliced scallions.

COOK'S TIP

Wash your hands after handling chilies, as their fiery seeds and flesh can cause painful burning.

Thai Chicken with Peanut Sauce

A favorite Thai dish, served with a spicy peanut sauce, that
can be made with chicken or beef.

Serves 4–6

4 skinless, boneless
chicken breasts

MARINADE

1 small onion,
finely chopped

1 garlic clove, crushed

1-inch piece fresh
ginger root, finely chopped

2 tbsp dark soy sauce

2 tsp chile powder

1 tsp ground coriander seeds

2 tsp dark brown sugar

1 tbsp lemon or lime juice

1 tbsp vegetable oil

SPICY PEANUT SAUCE

1¼ cups coconut milk

⅓ cup crunchy peanut butter

1 tbsp fish sauce

1 tsp lemon or lime juice

salt and pepper

1 Trim any fat from the chicken
breasts then cut the meat into thin
strips, about 3 inches long.

2 To make the marinade, place all the
ingredients in a shallow dish and mix
well. Add the chicken strips and turn
in the marinade until well coated.
Cover with plastic wrap and marinate
in the refrigerator for 2 hours or
overnight, if possible.

3 Remove the chicken from the
marinade and thread the pieces,
accordion style, on bamboo or other
thin wooden skewers.

4 Broil for 8–10 minutes, turning and
brushing occasionally with the
marinade, until cooked.

5 Meanwhile, to make the spicy
peanut sauce, mix the coconut milk
with the peanut butter, fish sauce, and
lemon or lime juice in a pan. Bring to a
boil and cook for 3 minutes. Season
with salt and pepper to taste and
serve the sauce with the cooked
chicken satay.

Chicken Satay Kabobs

Small kabobs of satay chicken with cubes of cheese and cherry tomatoes
are served on crisp lettuce leaves.

Makes 8
1 tbsp sherry
1 tbsp light soy sauce
1 tbsp sesame oil
finely grated rind of $^1/_2$ lemon
1 tbsp lemon or lime juice
2 tsp sesame seeds
1 pound skinless, boneless chicken breasts
$^3/_4$ cup brick cheese or Gouda cheese
16 cherry tomatoes
salt and pepper
crisp lettuce leaves, such as romaine, to serve

PEANUT DIP

$^1/_3$ cup shredded coconut
$^2/_3$ cup boiling water
$^1/_2$ cup crunchy peanut butter
pinch of chili powder
1 tsp brown sugar
1 tbsp light soy sauce
2 scallions, trimmed and chopped

1 Combine the sherry, soy sauce, sesame oil, lemon rind, lemon or lime juice, and sesame seeds in a bowl. Season to taste with salt and pepper.

2 Cut the chicken into 1-inch cubes. Add to the marinade and mix well to coat completely. Cover and chill for 3–6 hours.

3 To make the dip, put the coconut in a saucepan with the boiling water and bring back to a boil. Remove from the heat and set aside until cold.

4 Add the peanut butter, chili powder, sugar, and soy sauce and bring to a boil over low heat. Simmer gently, stirring, for 2–3 minutes, until thickened, then cool.

5 Soak eight wooden skewers in warm water for 30 minutes. When the dip mixture is cold, stir in the scallions. Turn into a serving bowl and set aside until required.

6 Thread the chicken onto the eight prepared wooden skewers. Cook under a moderate broiler for about 5 minutes on each side, until cooked through. Set aside until cold.

7 Cut the cheese into 16 cubes and add a cube and a cherry tomato to each end of the skewers.

8 Serve on lettuce with the dip.

Sticky Chicken Wings

These need to be eaten with your fingers, so serve
them at an informal supper.

Serves 4–6
1 small onion, finely chopped
2 garlic cloves, crushed
2 tbsp olive oil
2 cups sieved tomatoes
2 tsp dried thyme
1 tsp dried oregano
pinch of fennel seeds
3 tbsp red wine vinegar
2 tbsp Dijon mustard
pinch of ground cinnamon
2 tbsp brown sugar
1 tsp chili flakes
2 tbsp molasses
16 chicken wings
salt and pepper
celery and cherry tomatoes, to serve

1 Sauté the onion and garlic in the oil
for about 10 minutes, until softened
and translucent.

2 Add the sieved tomatoes, thyme,
oregano, fennel seeds, vinegar,
mustard, and cinnamon to the pan
with the sugar, chili flakes, and
molasses. Season to taste with salt
and pepper. Bring to a boil, then
reduce the heat, and simmer gently
for 15 minutes, until slightly reduced.

3 Put the chicken wings in a large
dish, and coat liberally with the sauce.
Marinade for 3 hours, or as long as
possible, stirring often.

4 Cook the chicken wings over a
medium hot barbecue for
15–20 minutes, or until crispy and
cooked through. Turn and baste
frequently with the marinade.

5 Serve piping hot with celery and
cherry tomatoes.

COOK'S VARIATION

Instead of molasses, use either
honey or maple syrup for a
different flavor and lighter color.

Crispy-Coated Rock Cornish Hens

You could adapt this recipe using a whole chicken or chicken pieces,
serving them on a bed of moist and colorful vegetables.

Serves 6
4 tbsp vegetable oil
¼ cup butter
6 small Rock Cornish hens, trussed
1 large onion, sliced
1 pound baby carrots
1 tbsp all-purpose flour
²/₃ cup white wine
juice of 2 oranges
2 fennel bulbs, quartered
1¼ cups chicken stock
½ tsp salt
1 tbsp black peppercorns, lightly crushed
1 tsp cornstarch
²/₃ cup thick unsweetened yogurt
salt and pepper

COATING
3 tbsp raw crystal sugar
1 tbsp black peppercorns, lightly crushed
3 tbsp coarse sea salt
²/₃ cup thick unsweetened yogurt

1 Heat the oil in a large skillet and add the butter. Add the Rock Cornish hens, in batches, and cook until golden. Remove and keep warm.

2 Add the onion to the skillet and sauté until translucent. Add the carrots, stir, then sprinkle with the flour, and blend well. Stir in the wine and orange juice. Add the fennel, stock, salt, and peppercorns. Bring to a boil, then pour into a roasting pan.

3 Add the Rock Cornish hens, cover with foil, and cook in a preheated oven at 400°F for 40 minutes.

4 To make the coating, stir together the sugar, peppercorns, salt, and yogurt to make a thick paste.

5 Preheat the broiler to high. Remove the Rock Cornish hens from the roasting pan and place them on a rack. Spread the paste evenly over the Rock Cornish hens, then broil for about 3–4 minutes, until the coating is crisp.

6 Arrange the drained vegetables on a warm serving dish. Place the roasting pan over medium heat and bring the sauce to a boil. Stir the cornstarch into the yogurt then blend into the sauce. Taste and adjust the seasoning, if necessary. Place the Rock Cornish hens in the center of the dish, spoon a little sauce over the vegetables, and serve the rest separately.

Broiled Chicken Salad

Broiling is a quick, healthy cooking method, ideal for sealing in the juices and flavor of chicken breasts, and a wonderful way to cook summer vegetables. Choose a good quality olive oil to enhance the fresh flavors to the fullest.

Serves 4
1 small eggplant, sliced
2 garlic cloves, crushed
finely grated rind of $1/2$ lemon
1 tbsp chopped fresh mint
6 tbsp olive oil, plus extra, to serve
4 boneless chicken breasts
2 medium zucchini, sliced
1 medium red bell pepper, seeded and quartered
1 small bulb fennel, thickly sliced
1 large red onion, thickly sliced
1 small ciabatta loaf or 1 French baguette, sliced
salt and pepper
salad, to serve

occasionally, until they are golden brown and tender, or cook on a ridged griddle pan on the hob. Brush the bread slices with olive oil and broil until golden.

5 Drizzle a little olive oil over the chicken and broiled vegetables and serve hot or cold with the crusty bread toasts and a salad.

1 Place the eggplant slices in a colander and sprinkle with salt. Leave over a bowl to drain for 30 minutes, then rinse, and pat dry with paper towels. Mix together the garlic, lemon rind, mint, and olive oil. Season to taste with salt and pepper.

2 Slash the chicken breasts at intervals with a sharp knife. Spoon about half of the seasoned oil mixture over them.

3 Combine the eggplants and the remaining vegetables, then toss in the remaining oil mixture. Marinate the chicken and vegetables for about 30 minutes.

4 Cook the chicken breasts and vegetables under a preheated broiler or over a medium barbecue, turning

Mustardy Barbecue Drummers

Great for barbecues, or for simple summer lunches and picnics,
this is an easy and tasty recipe for chicken drumsticks.

Serves 4
10 slices smoked bacon
1 garlic clove, crushed
3 tbsp wholegrain mustard
4 tbsp fresh brown bread crumbs
8 chicken drumsticks
1 tbsp sunflower oil

1 Chop and fry two of the bacon slices without additional fat for 3–4 minutes, stirring. Remove from the heat and stir in the garlic, 2 tablespoons of the mustard, and the bread crumbs.

2 Carefully loosen the skin from each drumstick. Spoon a little of the mustard stuffing under each, smoothing over firmly.

3 Wrap a bacon slice around each drumstick, and secure in place with toothpicks.

4 Mix together the remaining mustard and the oil, brush over the chicken and cook on a moderately hot barbecue or under preheated broiler for about 25 minutes, until there is no trace of pink in the juices when the chicken is pierced with the point of a sharp knife. Serve hot or cold.

COOK'S TIP

Do not cook the chicken over the hottest part of the barbecue or the outside may be charred before the center is cooked.

Skewered Spicy Tomato Chicken

These low-fat, spicy skewers are cooked in a matter of minutes—and they can be assembled ahead of time and stored in the refrigerator until you need them.

Serves 4
1 pound skinless, boneless chicken breasts
3 tbsp tomato paste
2 tbsp clear honey
2 tbsp Worcestershire sauce
1 tbsp chopped fresh rosemary
8 ounces cherry tomatoes
sprigs of rosemary, to garnish
couscous or boiled rice, to serve

1 Cut the chicken into 1-inch chunks and place in a bowl.

2 Mix together the tomato paste, honey, Worcestershire sauce, and rosemary. Add to the chicken, stirring to coat evenly.

3 Alternating the chicken pieces and tomatoes, thread them onto eight wooden skewers.

4 Spoon over any remaining glaze. Cook under a preheated broiler for 8–10 minutes, turning occasionally, until the chicken is thoroughly cooked. Serve on a bed of couscous or boiled rice, garnished with sprigs of fresh rosemary.

COOK'S TIP

Couscous is made from semolina that has been made into separate grains. It usually just needs moistening or steaming before serving.

Barbecued Chicken Quarters with Warm Aioli

Chicken quarters are barbecued, then served with a strongly flavored garlic mayonnaise, which originated in Provence, France.

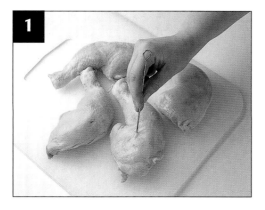

Serves 4
4 chicken quarters
2 tbsp oil
2 tbsp lemon juice
2 tsp dried thyme
salt and pepper

AIOLI
5 garlic cloves, crushed
2 egg yolks
$^1/_2$ cup olive oil
$^1/_2$ cup sunflower oil
2 tsp lemon juice
2 tbsp boiling water

1 Using a skewer, prick the chicken quarters in several places, then place them in a shallow dish.

2 Mix the oil, lemon juice, thyme, and seasoning together, then pour over the chicken. Turn the chicken quarters to ensure they are well coated with the marinade. Set aside for 2 hours.

3 To make the aioli, put the garlic in a bowl with a pinch of salt and beat together to make a paste. Beat in the egg yolks. Add the olive and sunflower oils, drop by drop, beating vigorously, until the mayonnaise becomes creamy and smooth. Add the oils in a thin steady trickle and continue beating until the aioli is thick. Stir in the lemon juice and season with pepper. Set aside in a warm place.

4 Place the chicken on a moderate barbecue and cook for about

25–30 minutes. Brush with the marinade and turn the portions so that they cook evenly. Remove and arrange on a serving plate.

5 Beat the water into the aioli and turn into a warm serving bowl. Serve with the chicken.

COOK'S TIP

To make a quick aioli, add the garlic to $1^1/_4$ cups good-quality mayonnaise, then place in a bowl over a pan of warm water and beat together. Just before serving add 1–2 tablespoons of hot water.

Skewered Chicken with Bramble Sauce

This fall recipe can be made with fresh-picked wild blackberries from the hedgerow if you are lucky enough to have a good supply.

Serves 4
4 chicken breasts or 8 thighs
4 tbsp dry white wine or cider
2 tbsp chopped fresh rosemary
pepper
rosemary sprigs and blackberries, to garnish

SAUCE
scant 2 cups blackberries
1 tbsp cider vinegar
2 tbsp red currant jelly
1/4 tsp grated nutmeg

6 Spoon a little bramble sauce onto each plate and place a chicken skewer on top. Sprinkle with nutmeg and serve hot, garnished with rosemary and blackberries.

COOK'S TIP

If you use canned fruit, omit the red currant jelly.

1 Cut the chicken into 1-inch pieces and place in a bowl. Sprinkle the wine and rosemary over them and season well with pepper. Cover and marinate for at least an hour.

2 Drain the marinade from the chicken and thread the meat onto 8 metal or wooden skewers.

3 Cook under a preheated broiler for 8–10 minutes, turning occasionally, until golden and evenly cooked.

4 Meanwhile, to make the sauce, place the marinade in a pan with the blackberries and simmer gently until soft. Press though a strainer.

5 Return to the pan, add the cider vinegar and red currant jelly, and bring to a boil. Boil uncovered until the sauce has reduced by about one third.

Chicken Cajun-Style

These spicy chicken wings are good served with a chili salsa and salad.

Serves 4
16 chicken wings
4 tsp paprika
2 tsp ground coriander
1 tsp celery salt
1 tsp ground cumin
$\frac{1}{2}$ tsp cayenne
$\frac{1}{2}$ tsp salt
1 tbsp oil
2 tbsp red wine vinegar

1 Wash the chicken wings and pat dry with paper towels. Remove the wing tips.

2 Mix together the paprika, coriander, celery salt, cumin, cayenne, salt, oil, and vinegar.

3 Rub this mixture over the wings and set aside in the refrigerator for a least 1 hour to allow the flavors to permeate the chicken.

4 Cook the wings on a moderate barbecue, occasionally brushing with oil, for about 15 minutes, turning often, until cooked through. Transfer to a serving dish and serve immediately.

COOK'S TIP

To save time, you can buy ready-made Cajun spice seasoning to rub over the chicken wings.

Chicken with Garden Herbs

Warm weather calls for lighter eating, and this chilled chicken dish in a subtle herb vinaigrette is ideal for a summer dinner party or for a picnic. The chicken can be cooked several hours before you need it and stored in the refrigerator until required.

Serves 4
4 part-boned, skinless chicken breasts
6 tbsp olive oil
2 tbsp lemon juice
4 tbsp finely chopped summer herbs, such as parsley, chives, and mint
1 ripe avocado
1/2 cup ricotta
pepper

1 Using a sharp knife, cut 3–4 deep slashes in the chicken breasts.

2 Place in a flameproof dish and brush lightly with a little of the olive oil. Cook the chicken under a preheated broiler, until it is golden and the juices run clear when the it is pierced with the point of a sharp knife. Turn once during cooking.

3 Combine the remaining oil with the lemon juice and herbs and season with pepper. Spoon the oil over the chicken and set aside to cool. Chill for at least 1 hour.

4 Mash the avocado or process in a food processor with the ricotta. Season with pepper to taste. Serve the chicken with the avocado sauce.

Ginger Chicken & Corn

Chicken wings and corn in a sticky ginger marinade are designed to be eaten with the fingers—there is no other way! The corn has a delicious nutty texture, and if fresh corn is unavailable, you can use thawed, frozen corn instead.

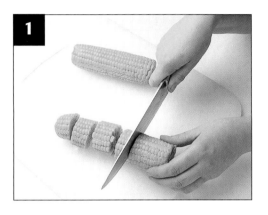

Serves 6
3 fresh corn cobs
12 chicken wings
1-inch piece fresh ginger root
6 tbsp lemon juice
4 tsp sunflower oil
1 tbsp golden superfine sugar
baked potatoes or salad, serve

1 Remove the husks and silks from the corn and cut each cob into 6 slices. Place in a large bowl with the chicken wings.

2 Peel and grate the ginger or chop finely. Mix together with the lemon juice, oil, and sugar, then toss with the corn and chicken to coat.

3 Thread the corn and wings onto skewers to make turning easier.

4 Cook under a preheated broiler or over a moderate barbecue for 15–20 minutes, basting with the gingery glaze and turning frequently, until the corn is golden brown and tender and the chicken is cooked. Serve with baked potatoes or salad.

COOK'S TIP

Cut off the wing tips before broiling, as they burn very easily. Or you can cover them with small pieces of foil.

Skewered Chicken Spirals

These unusual chicken kabobs have a wonderful Mediterranean flavor, and the bacon helps keep them moist during cooking. They are quite easy to assemble, and can be made earlier in the day and refrigerated until needed.

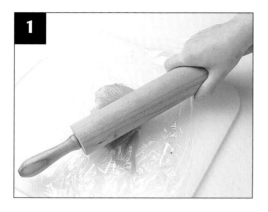

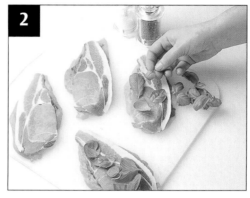

Serves 4
4 skinless, boneless chicken breasts
1 garlic clove, crushed
2 tbsp tomato paste
4 slices smoked bacon
large handful fresh basil leaves
oil for brushing
salt and pepper
salad greens, for serving

1 Spread out a piece of chicken between two sheets of plastic wrap and beat firmly with a rolling pin to flatten the chicken to an even thickness. Repeat with the remaining chicken breasts.

2 Mix the garlic and tomato paste and spread it over the chicken. Lay a bacon slice over each, then scatter with the fresh basil. Season well with salt and pepper.

3 Roll up each piece of chicken firmly, then cut into thick slices.

4 Thread the slices onto four skewers, making sure the skewer holds the chicken in a spiral shape.

5 Brush lightly with oil and cook over a hot barbecue or under a preheated broiler for about 10 minutes, turning once. Serve hot with salad greens.

Broiled Rock Cornish Hens with Lemon & Tarragon

Butterflied Rock Cornish hens are complemented by the delicate fragrance of lemon and tarragon and broiled.

Serves 2
2 Rock Cornish hens
4 sprigs fresh tarragon
1 tsp oil
2 tbsp butter
rind of $1/2$ lemon
1 tbsp lemon juice
1 garlic clove
salt and pepper
tarragon and orange slices, to garnish
new potatoes, to serve

1 Prepare the Rock Cornish hens, turn them breast-side down on a chopping board and cut them through the backbone. Crush each bird gently to break the bones so that they lie flat while cooking. Season each with salt to taste.

2 Turn them over and insert a sprig of tarragon under the skin over each side of the breast.

3 Brush the Rock Cornish hens with oil and place under a preheated broiler. Broil for about 15 minutes, turning half way through the cooking time, until lightly browned.

4 Meanwhile, to make the glaze, melt the butter in a small saucepan, add the lemon rind, lemon juice, and garlic and season to taste with salt and pepper.

5 Brush the Rock Cornish hens with the glaze, and cook for a further 15 minutes, turning them once and brushing regularly so that they stay moist. Garnish the Rock Cornish hens with tarragon and orange slices and serve with new potatoes.

COOK'S TIP

Once the Rock Cornish hens are flattened, insert 2 metal skewers through them to keep them flat.

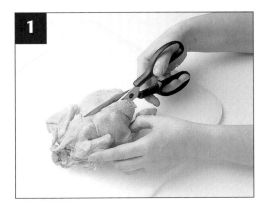

Tropical Chicken Skewers

Chicken is given a Caribbean flavor. The marinade keeps them moist and succulent during cooking.

Serves 6
1½ pounds skinless, boneless chicken breasts
2 tbsp medium sherry
3 mangoes
bay leaves
2 tbsp oil
2 tbsp coarsely shredded coconut
pepper
salad greens, to serve

1 Cut the chicken into 1-inch cubes and toss them in the sherry, with a little pepper.

2 Cut the mangoes into 1-inch cubes, discarding the pit and skin.

3 Thread the chicken, mango cubes, and bay leaves alternately onto long skewers, then lightly brush all over with oil.

4 Broil the skewers under a preheated broiler for 8–10 minutes, turning occasionally, until golden. Sprinkle with the coconut and broil for a further 30 seconds. Serve the kabobs hot with crisp salad greens.

COOK'S TIP

Use mangoes that are ripe, but still firm, so that they hold together on the skewers during cooking. Another firm fruit that would be suitable is pineapple.

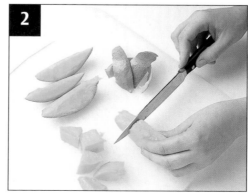

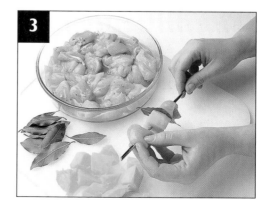

Spicy Sesame Chicken

This is a quick and easy recipe for the broiler, perfect
for lunch or to eat outdoors on a picnic.

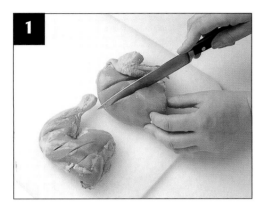

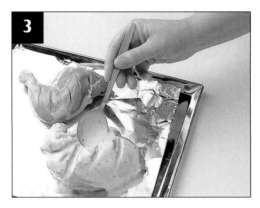

Serves 4
4 chicken quarters
1/2 cup unsweetened yogurt
finely grated rind and juice of 1 small lemon
2 tsp medium-hot curry paste
1 tbsp sesame seeds
lemon wedges, to garnish
salad and nan bread, to serve

1 Remove the skin from the chicken
and slash the flesh at intervals with a
sharp knife.

2 Mix together the yogurt, lemon
rind, lemon juice, and curry paste.

3 Spread the mixture over the
chicken and arrange on a foil-lined
broiler pan or cookie sheet.

4 Place under a preheated broiler and
broil for 12–15 minutes, turning once.
Alternatively, cook over a moderate
barbecue for 12–15 minutes. Broil
until golden brown and thoroughly
cooked. Just before the end of the
cooking time, sprinkle the chicken
with the sesame seeds. Serve,
garnished with lemon wedges and
with a salad and nan bread.

COOK'S VARIATION

Poppy seeds, fennel seeds,
or cumin seeds, or a mixture of all
three, can also be used to sprinkle
over the chicken.

Broiled Chicken with Pesto Toasts

This Italian-style dish is richly flavored with pesto, which is a mixture of basil, olive oil, pine nuts, and Parmesan cheese. Either red or green pesto can be used for this recipe. Sieved tomatoes are available in cans and jars.

Serves 4
8 part-boned chicken thighs
olive oil, for brushing
1$^2/_3$ cups sieved tomatoes
$^1/_2$ cup green or red pesto sauce
12 slices French bread
1 cup freshly grated Parmesan cheese
$^1/_2$ cup pine nuts or slivered almonds
basil sprig, to garnish

1 Arrange the chicken in a single layer in a wide flameproof dish and brush lightly with oil. Place under a preheated broiler for about 15 minutes, turning occasionally, until golden brown.

2 Pierce with the point of a sharp knife to ensure that the juices run clear and that the chicken is cooked.

3 Pour off any excess fat. Warm the sieved tomatoes and half the pesto sauce in a small pan and pour onto the chicken. Broil for a few more minutes, turning until coated.

4 Meanwhile, spread the remaining pesto onto the slices of bread. Arrange the bread over the chicken and sprinkle with the Parmesan cheese. Scatter the pine nuts over the cheese. Broil for 2–3 minutes, until browned and bubbling. Serve hot, garnished with a basil sprig.

Minty Lime Chicken

These tangy lime- and honey-coated pieces have a matching sauce
or dip based on creamy unsweetened yogurt. They could be served at a barbecue
or as a main course for a dinner party.

Serves 6
3 tbsp finely chopped mint
4 tbsp clear honey
4 tbsp lime juice
12 boneless chicken thighs
salt and pepper
salad, to serve

SAUCE
$^1\!/_2$ cup thick unsweetened yogurt
1 tbsp finely chopped mint
2 tsp finely grated lime rind

1 Combine the mint, honey, and lime juice in a bowl.

2 Use toothpicks to keep the chicken thighs in neat shapes and add the chicken to the marinade, turning to coat evenly.

3 Marinate for at least 30 minutes. Cook the chicken over a moderately hot barbecue or under a preheated broiler, turning frequently and basting with the marinade. The chicken is cooked if the juices run clear when the chicken is pierced with the point of a sharp knife.

4 Meanwhile, mix together all the ingredients for the sauce.

5 Remove the toothpicks and serve the chicken with a salad and the sauce for dipping or pouring.

Chicken Tikka & Mango Kabobs

Chicken tikka is one of the lower-fat dishes from India. Recipes vary and you can try your own combination of spices to suit your personal taste.

Serves 4
4 skinless, boneless, chicken breasts, cut into 1-inch cubes
1 garlic clove, crushed
1 tsp grated fresh ginger root
1 fresh green chili, seeded and finely chopped
6 tbsp reduced fat unsweetened yogurt
1 tbsp tomato paste
1 tsp ground cumin seeds
1 tsp ground coriander seeds
1 tsp ground turmeric
1 large ripe mango
1 tbsp lime juice
salt and pepper
fresh cilantro leaves, to garnish

TO SERVE
boiled white rice
lime wedges
mixed salad
warmed nan bread

1 Place the chicken in a shallow dish.

2 Mix together the garlic, ginger, chili, yogurt, tomato paste, cumin, coriander, turmeric, and salt and pepper. Spoon onto the chicken, mix well, cover, and chill for 2 hours.

3 Slice down either side of the mango pit and cut the flesh into cubes. Toss in the lime juice, then cover, and chill until required.

4 Thread the chicken and mango pieces onto skewers. Place them on a broiler rack and brush the chicken

with the yogurt marinade and any remaining lime juice.

5 Cook under a preheated broiler for 6–7 minutes on each side, brushing once with the marinade, until the chicken juices run clear when the

cubes are pierced with the point of a sharp knife.

6 Serve on a bed of rice on a warm platter with fresh cilantro leaves, lime wedges, a mixed salad, and warm nan bread.

Sweet & Sour Drumsticks

Chicken drumsticks are marinated to impart a tangy, sweet and sour flavor and a shiny glaze.

Serves 4
8 chicken drumsticks
4 tbsp red wine vinegar
2 tbsp tomato paste
2 tbsp soy sauce
2 tbsp clear honey
1 tbsp Worcestershire sauce
1 garlic clove
pinch of cayenne pepper
salt and pepper
salad, to serve

1 Skin the chicken, if desired, and slash 2–3 times with a sharp knife.

2 Put the chicken drumsticks into a nonmetallic container.

3 Mix together all the remaining ingredients and pour onto the chicken, turning to coat thoroughly.

4 Marinate in the refrigerator for 1 hour. Cook the drumsticks on a moderate barbecue for about 20 minutes, brushing with the marinade and turning during cooking. Serve with a crisp salad.

COOK'S TIP

For a tangy flavor, add the juice of 1 lime to the marinade. While the drumsticks are broiling, check regularly to ensure that they are not burning.

Hot & Spicy

Because chicken is popular throughout the world, there are countless spicy recipes from Asia, Mexico, Southeast Asia, the Caribbean, Spain, and Japan. Lime juice, cilantro, fish sauce, and fresh ginger root add the authentic tastes of Thailand to Thai-style Chicken Fried Rice, while Bang-Bang Chicken is a popular Szechuan dish from China with a sauce made from

peanuts and sesame seeds. From Mexico comes Enchilada Layers—tortillas stacked up with layers of tomato

sauce and spicy chicken—and Chicken Fajitas—chicken spiked with hot chilies, served in tortillas, and topped with sour cream, red onion, and limes. Add Margueritas and you have a tasty Mexican spread. Rock Cornish hens with Green Peppercorns is a creative modern dish that would be perfect for any special occasion. It is served with rice cooked in a tasty sauce of peppercorns, mustard and wine.

Bang-Bang Chicken

The cooked chicken meat is tenderized by being pounded with a rolling pin,
hence the name for this very popular Szechuan dish from China.

Serves 4
4 cups water
2 chicken quarters
(breast half and leg)
1 cucumber,
cut into matchstick shreds

SAUCE
2 tbsp light soy sauce
1 tsp sugar
1 tbsp finely chopped scallions
1 tsp red chili oil
1/4 tsp pepper
1 tsp white sesame seeds
2 tbsp peanut butter, creamed
with a little sesame oil

1 Bring the water to a rolling boil in a wok or a large saucepan. Add the chicken pieces, reduce the heat, cover, and cook for 30–35 minutes.

2 Remove the chicken from the pan and immerse it in a bowl of cold water for at least 1 hour to cool it, ready for shredding.

3 Remove the chicken pieces and drain well. Pat dry with paper towels, then take the meat off the bone.

4 On a flat surface, pound the chicken with a rolling pin, then tear the meat into shreds with two forks. Mix with the shredded cucumber, and arrange in a serving dish.

5 To serve, mix together all the sauce ingredients and pour onto the chicken and cucumber.

Thai-Style Chicken Fried Rice

A few special ingredients give this rice dish an authentic Thai flavor.

Serves 4
generous 1 cup white long-grain rice
4 tbsp vegetable oil
2 garlic cloves, finely chopped
6 shallots, finely sliced
1 red bell pepper, seeded and diced
4 ounces green beans, cut into 1-inch lengths
1 tbsp Thai red curry paste
12 ounces cooked skinless, boneless chicken, chopped
$1/2$ tsp ground coriander seeds
1 tsp finely grated fresh ginger root
2 tbsp Thai fish sauce
finely grated rind of 1 lime
3 tbsp lime juice
1 tbsp chopped fresh cilantro
salt and pepper

TO GARNISH

lime wedges
sprigs of fresh cilantro

1 Cook the rice in plenty of boiling, lightly salted water for 12–15 minutes, until tender. Drain, rinse in cold water, and drain thoroughly.

2 Heat the oil in a large skillet or wok and add the garlic and shallots. Fry gently for 2–3 minutes until golden.

3 Add the bell pepper and green beans and stir-fry for 2 minutes. Add the Thai curry paste and stir-fry for 1 minute.

4 Add the cooked rice to the pan, then the chicken, ground coriander, ginger, fish sauce, lime rind and juice, and fresh cilantro. Stir-fry over a medium high heat for about 4–5 minutes, until the rice and chicken are thoroughly reheated. Season to taste with salt and pepper.

5 Transfer to a warm serving dish, garnish with lime wedges and cilantro, and serve immediately.

Chicken Fajitas

This spicy chicken filling, made with mixed bell peppers, chilies, and mushrooms and strongly flavored with lime, is served in folded tortillas and topped with sour cream.
Many other fillings can be used—the possibilities are endless.

Serves 4
2 red bell peppers
2 green bell peppers
2 tbsp olive oil
2 onions, chopped
3 garlic cloves, crushed
1 chili, seeded and finely chopped
2 skinless, boneless chicken breasts, about 12 ounces
2 ounces button mushrooms, sliced
2 tsp chopped fresh cilantro
grated rind of $\frac{1}{2}$ lime
2 tbsp lime juice
4 wheat or corn tortillas
4–6 tbsp sour cream
salt and pepper

TO GARNISH

sliced red onion
chopped tomatoes
lime wedges

1 Halve the bell peppers, remove the core and seeds, and place skin side upward, under a preheated broiler until well charred. Cool slightly and then peel off the skin. Cut the flesh into thin slices.

2 Heat the oil in a skillet, add the onions, garlic, and chili, and sauté gently for a few minutes until the onion has softened.

3 Cut the chicken into narrow strips. Add to the vegetable mixture in the skillet and fry, stirring occasionally, for 4–5 minutes, until almost cooked.

4 Add the bell peppers, mushrooms, chopped cilantro, lime rind and juice, and continue to cook, stirring occasionally, for 2–3 minutes. Season to taste with salt and pepper.

5 Heat the tortillas, wrapped in foil, in a preheated oven at 350°F for a few minutes. Bend them in half and divide the chicken mixture among them.

6 Top the chicken filling with a spoonful of sour cream. Serve garnished with red onion slices, chopped tomatoes, and lime wedges.

Enchilada Layers

You can vary the filling for these layered Mexican tortillas by using beef,
fish, or shellfish. If desired, the tortillas can be rolled up once they are filled,
rather than baking them in layers.

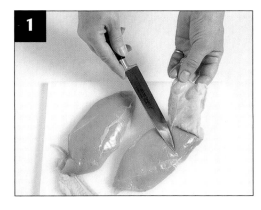

Serves 4
1 pound boneless chicken breasts
2 tbsp olive oil
1 large onion, thinly sliced
3 garlic cloves, crushed
1 tsp ground cumin seeds
2 tbsp stock or water
1 tbsp chopped fresh cilantro
6 wheat or corn tortillas
3/4 cup coarsely grated feta cheese
salt and pepper
sprigs of fresh cilantro, to garnish

TOMATO SAUCE

2 tbsp oil
1 onion, very finely chopped
3 garlic cloves, crushed
1 red chili, finely chopped
14 ounce can chopped tomatoes with herbs
7 ounce can chopped tomatoes
3 tbsp tomato paste
2 tbsp lime juice
2 tsp superfine sugar
salt and pepper

1 Remove the skin from the chicken
and chop the flesh finely. Heat the oil
and sauté the onion and garlic until
softened and translucent.

2 Add the chicken and fry for
5 minutes. Add the cumin and stock.
Cook for 3 minutes, until tender. Add
the cilantro. Remove from the heat.

3 To make the tomato sauce, heat the
oil over low heat and sauté the onion,
garlic and chili gently over low heat
until softened.

4 Add all the tomatoes, the tomato
paste, lime juice, and sugar, and
seasoning. Simmer gently for
10 minutes.

5 Cover a tortilla with ¹/₅ of the
chicken mixture and 2 tablespoons of
the tomato sauce, then sprinkle with

grated cheese. Continue to layer in
this way, finishing with cheese.

6 Place the layered enchiladas in a
dish in a preheated oven, at 375°F for
25 minutes, or until the top is lightly
browned. Serve in wedges, garnished
with a sprig of cilantro.

Chicken Burritos

A filling of chopped chicken, scrambled eggs, together with a spicy pumpkin seed, herb and yogurt mixture, and sliced tomatoes, is rolled into wheat or corn tortillas.

Serves 4
¹/₂ cup pumpkin seeds
3–4 scallions, trimmed and sliced
1 chili, seeded and finely chopped
4 tbsp chopped fresh flat leaf parsley
1 tbsp chopped fresh cilantro
6 tbsp unsweetened yogurt
4 wheat or corn tortillas
2 tbsp butter
4 tbsp milk
1 garlic clove, crushed
6 eggs, lightly beaten
4 ounces cooked skinless, boneless chicken, shredded
2 tomatoes, peeled and sliced
salt and pepper

TO GARNISH

shredded lettuce
sliced red onions
chopped tomatoes

1 Dry-fry the pumpkin seeds lightly in a heavy-based skillet. Finely chop, then put into a food processor with the scallions and chile, and process. Alternatively, pound in a mortar with a pestle.

2 Add the chopped parsley and cilantro, followed by the yogurt, and blend until well mixed. Season to taste with salt and pepper.

3 Wrap the tortillas in foil and warm for a few minutes in a preheated oven at 350°F.

4 Melt the butter with the milk and garlic and season to taste with salt

and pepper. Remove from the heat and stir in the eggs. Cook over low heat, stirring, until just scrambled. Stir in the chicken.

5 Lay the tortillas flat and spoon some scrambled egg down the center of each. Top the scrambled egg with

the pumpkin seed mixture, then add the sliced tomatoes.

6 Roll up the tortillas and serve, garnished with the shredded lettuce, sliced red onions, and tomatoes.

Chicken Paprika

Paprika, caraway seeds and sour cream give this dish an Eastern European flavor.
Paprika is a seasoning commonly used in Hungary.

Serves 4
4 tbsp butter
4 chicken quarters
1 tbsp paprika
1 tbsp caraway seeds
1 onion, finely chopped
1 clove garlic, crushed
1 red bell pepper, seeded and finely chopped
1½ cups finely chopped mushrooms
⅔ cup diced pancetta, or smoked bacon
⅓ cup sherry
⅔ cup sour cream
1 tbsp cornstarch
salt and pepper

1 Heat the butter in a skillet, add the chicken, and brown well on all sides. Stir in the paprika and caraway seeds and season to taste. Remove the chicken and set aside.

2 Add the onion and garlic to the skillet and sauté in the butter for about 10 minutes. Transfer the chicken and onions to an ovenproof dish, cover, and transfer to a preheated oven at 400°F. Bake for 40 minutes, turning once or twice.

3 Remove the chicken and onions from the dish, reserving the cooking juices. Set aside and keep warm. Pour the cooking juices into a large skillet set over a moderate heat.

4 Stir in the bell pepper, mushrooms, and pancetta or bacon, and fry for 15 minutes.

5 Add the sherry, and simmer until reduced. Season to taste.

6 To finish the sauce, combine the sour cream and cornstarch to make a smooth paste and stir into the skillet until the sauce is smooth and thick. Taste and adjust the seasoning if necessary. Serve the chicken pieces with the sauce.

Chicken, Cilantro, Ginger, & Lemon Stir-fry

The sweet and sour flavors in this recipe add a Chinese touch to this Indian stir-fry.
The dish can be served cold in the summer with a spicy rice salad or a lettuce salad.

Serves 4
3 tbsp oil
1¹/₂ pounds skinless, boneless chicken breasts, cut into 2-inch strips
3 garlic cloves, crushed
1¹/₂-inch piece fresh ginger root, cut into strips
1 tsp pomegranate seeds, crushed
¹/₂ tsp ground turmeric
1 tsp garam masala
2 fresh green chilies, sliced
¹/₂ tsp salt
4 tbsp lemon juice
grated rind of 1 lemon
6 tbsp chopped fresh cilantro
¹/₂ cup chicken stock
nan bread, to serve

1 Heat the oil in a wok or large skillet and stir-fry the chicken until golden brown all over. Remove from the skillet and set aside.

2 Add the garlic, ginger, and pomegranate seeds to the skillet and fry in the oil for 1 minute.

3 Stir in the turmeric, garam masala, and chilies, and fry for 30 seconds.

4 Return the chicken to the skillet and add the salt, lemon juice, lemon rind, cilantro, and stock. Stir the chicken to ensure it is thoroughly coated in the sauce.

5 Bring to a boil, then lower the heat, and simmer for 10–15 minutes, until the chicken juices run clear when the thickest part of the chicken is pierced with the point of a sharp knife. Transfer to a warm serving dish and serve immediately with nan bread.

COOK'S TIP

If you cannot find pomegranate seeds, look for canned pomegranate juice instead, and use 2 teaspoons in the recipe.

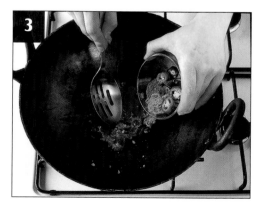

Chicken with Mushrooms

Try to find Chinese straw mushrooms for this dish. When cooked they are brown and slippery and make a delicious addition to the chicken.

Serves 4
10–12 ounces skinless, boneless chicken
¹/₂ tsp sugar
1 tbsp light soy sauce
1 tsp Chinese rice wine or dry sherry
2 tsp cornstarch
4–6 dried Chinese mushrooms, soaked in warm water and drained
1 tbsp finely shredded fresh ginger root
a few drops of sesame oil
salt and pepper
cilantro leaves, to garnish

1 Cut the chicken into bite-size pieces and place in a bowl. Add the sugar, soy sauce, Chinese rice wine or sherry, and cornstarch and marinate for 25–30 minutes.

2 Dry the mushrooms on paper towels. Slice into thin shreds, discarding any hard pieces of stem.

3 Place the chicken pieces on a heat-proof dish that will fit inside a bamboo steamer. Arrange the mushroom and ginger shreds on top of the chicken and sprinkle with sesame oil, and salt and pepper.

4 Place the dish on the rack inside a steamer or on a rack in a wok or large skillet filled with hot water. Steam over a high heat for 20 minutes. Serve hot, garnished with cilantro leaves.

Chicken with Bell Peppers

Sugar snap peas or celery can also be used in this spicy
Szechuan recipe to add extra crunchiness.

Serves 4

10 ounces skinless, boneless
chicken breasts

1 tsp salt

$^1\!/_2$ egg white

2 tsp cornstarch
mixed to a paste
with 3 tsp cold water

1 green bell pepper,
seeded and halved

$1^1\!/_4$ cups vegetable oil

1 scallion, finely shredded

a few strips of fresh ginger
root, thinly shredded

1–2 red chilies, seeded
and thinly shredded

$^1\!/_2$ tsp sugar

1 tbsp Chinese rice wine
or dry sherry

a few drops of sesame oil

1 Cut the chicken breast into strips,
then mix in a bowl with a pinch of
the salt, the egg white, and the
cornstarch paste.

2 Cut the bell pepper into thin
shreds about the same thickness
and length as the chicken strips.
Set aside.

3 Heat the vegetable oil in a
preheated wok or skillet, and deep-fry
the chicken strips, in batches, for
about 1 minute, or until the chicken
becomes golden brown and the strips
are well sealed. Remove the chicken
strips from the wok or skillet with a
slotted spoon, drain well, set aside,
and keep warm.

4 Carefully pour off the excess oil,
leaving about 1 tablespoon in the wok.
Add the scallion, ginger, chilies, and
bell pepper. Stir-fry for about
1 minute, then return the chicken to
the wok, together with the remaining
salt, the sugar, and the Chinese rice
wine or sherry. Stir-fry for another
minute, sprinkle with sesame oil,
transfer to a serving dish, and serve.

Quick Chinese Chicken with Noodles

Chicken and fresh vegetables are flavored with ginger and Chinese five-spice powder in this quick and easy stir-fry. Vary the vegetables according to what is in season and make sure that they are as fresh as possible.

Serves 4
6 ounces Chinese thread egg noodles
2 tbsp sesame or vegetable oil
¼ cup peanuts
1 bunch of scallions, sliced
1 green bell pepper, seeded and cut into thin strips
1 large carrot, cut into matchstick strips
1 cup cauliflower, broken into small flowerets
12 ounces skinless, boneless chicken, cut into strips
3 cups sliced mushrooms
1 tsp finely grated fresh ginger root
1 tsp Chinese five-spice powder
1 tbsp chopped fresh cilantro
1 tbsp light soy sauce
salt and pepper
fresh chives, to garnish

1 Put the noodles into a large bowl and cover with boiling water. Set aside to soak for 6 minutes, or according to the instructions on the packet.

2 Meanwhile, heat the oil in a preheated wok or large skillet. Add the peanuts and stir-fry for about 1 minute, until browned. Lift the peanuts out with a slotted spoon and drain on paper towels.

3 Add the scallions, bell pepper, carrot, cauliflower flowerets, and chicken strips to the wok or skillet. Stir-fry over high heat for about

4–5 minutes, until the chicken is golden brown and cooked thoroughly. The vegetables should be still crisp, bright, and colorful.

4 Drain the noodles thoroughly and add them to the wok. Add the mushrooms and stir-fry for 2 minutes.

Add the grated ginger, five-spice powder, and cilantro and stir-fry for another minute.

5 Season with the soy sauce and salt and pepper. Sprinkle with the peanuts, garnish with chives, and serve at once on warm plates.

Lime & Cilantro Chicken Fried Rice

Lime rind and lime juice are combined with chopped fresh cilantro
to give this dish a lively Thai flavor.

Serves 4
generous 1 cup long–grain white rice
4 tbsp vegetable oil
2 garlic cloves, finely chopped
1 small green chili, seeded and finely chopped
5 shallots, finely sliced
1 tbsp Thai green curry paste
1 yellow or green bell pepper, seeded and chopped
2 celery stalks, finely sliced
$1^1/_2$ cups chopped cooked skinless, boneless chicken
2 tbsp light soy sauce
finely grated rind of 1 lime
2 tbsp lime juice
1 tbsp chopped fresh cilantro
$^1/_4$ cup unsalted peanuts, toasted
TO GARNISH
sprigs of fresh cilantro
finely sliced shallots
lime slices

1 Cook the rice in plenty of boiling, lightly salted water for about 12 minutes, until tender. Drain, rinse with cold water, and drain thoroughly again.

2 Heat the oil in a preheated wok or large skillet and add the garlic. Fry gently for 2 minutes until golden. Add the chili and shallots and cook, stirring, for a further 3–4 minutes, until slightly softened.

3 Add the Thai curry paste to the wok or skillet and fry for 1 minute, then add the yellow or green bell pepper and the celery. Stir-fry briskly for 2 minutes.

4 Add the cooked rice to the wok or skillet and add the chicken, soy sauce, lime rind and juice, and cilantro. Stir-fry over a medium-high heat for about 4–5 minutes, until the rice and chicken are heated through.

5 Transfer to a warm serving dish and sprinkle with peanuts. Garnish with sprigs of fresh cilantro, shallots, and lime slices and serve.

Rock Cornish Hens with Peppercorns

Baby chickens are a good alternative to chicken. One bird serves two people and can be cooked whole. Sautéed cherry tomatoes are a colorful accompaniment.

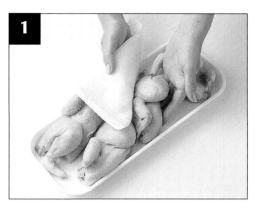

Serves 4
2 Rock Cornish hens, halved, washed, and dried
2 tbsp oil
2 tbsp butter
1 onion, chopped
3 tbsp bottled green peppercorns
2 tbsp wholegrain mustard
$\frac{1}{2}$ cup white wine
1$\frac{1}{3}$ cups basmati and wild rice
2 cups chicken stock
salt and pepper

1 Wash the Rock Cornish hens and pat dry with paper towels. Heat the oil and butter, and cook the onion for 5 minutes, until softened.

2 Season the Rock Cornish hens well with salt and pepper, and add to the pan. Brown all over, then transfer to a cookie sheet.

3 Finish cooking the Rock Cornish hens in a preheated oven at 400°F for 30 minutes.

4 Meanwhile, stir the peppercorns, mustard, and wine into the pan juices, bring to a boil, and then reduce by half.

5 Stir in the rice and pour in the stock. Season to taste with salt and pepper and bring to simmering point. Cook for 18–20 minutes. Adjust the seasoning, if necessary.

6 Serve the Rock Cornish hens piping hot on a bed of rice.

Spicy Chicken Tortillas

Serve these easy-to-prepare tortillas to friends or as a special family supper.
The chicken filling has a mild, mellow spicy heat and a fresh salad makes
a perfect accompaniment.

Serves 4
2 tbsp oil
8 skinless, boneless chicken thighs, sliced
1 onion, chopped
2 garlic cloves, chopped
1 tsp cumin seeds, roughly crushed
2 large dried chilies, sliced
14 ounce can tomatoes
14 ounce can red kidney beans, drained
$2/3$ cup chicken stock
2 tsp sugar
salt and pepper
lime wedges, to garnish
TO SERVE
1 large ripe avocado
1 lime
8 soft tortillas
1 cup thick unsweetened yogurt

1 Heat the oil in a large skillet or preheated wok, add the chicken and fry for 3 minutes. Add the onion and fry for 5 minutes, stirring until browned. Add the garlic, cumin and chilies, with their seeds, and cook for about 1 minute.

2 Add the tomatoes, kidney beans, chicken stock, and sugar. Season to taste with salt and pepper. Bring to a boil, breaking up the tomatoes. Cover and simmer for 15 minutes. Remove the lid and cook, stirring occasionally, for 5 minutes, or until the sauce has thickened.

3 Halve the avocado, discard the pit, and scoop out the flesh onto a plate. Mash the avocado with a fork. Cut half of the lime into 8 thin wedges. Squeeze the juice from the remaining lime over the avocado.

4 Warm the tortillas as the pack directs. Put two tortillas on each serving plate, fill with the chicken mixture, and top with spoonfuls of avocado and yogurt. Garnish the tortillas with lime wedges.

Kashmiri Chicken

This warming, rich, and spicy dish is based on the traditional cooking style of Northern India, using chicken on the bone. If desired, use boneless chicken breasts instead of legs, and cut into large chunks for cooking.

Serves 4
4 skinless chicken drumsticks
4 skinless chicken thighs
$^2/_3$ cup unsweetened yogurt
4 tbsp tikka curry paste
2 tbsp sunflower oil
1 medium onion, thinly sliced
1 garlic clove, crushed
1 tsp ground cumin
1 tsp finely chopped fresh ginger root
$^1/_2$ tsp chili paste
4 tsp chicken stock
2 tbsp ground almonds
salt
fresh cilantro, to garnish
pilau rice, pickles, and poppadums, to serve

1 Slash the chicken fairly deeply at intervals with a sharp knife and place in a large bowl.

2 Mix together the yogurt and curry paste and stir into the chicken, tossing to coat evenly. Cover and chill for at least 1 hour.

3 Heat the oil in a large skillet and fry the onion and garlic for 4–5 minutes, until softened, but not browned.

4 Stir in the cumin, ginger, and chili paste and cook gently for 1 minute.

5 Add the chicken pieces and fry gently, turning occasionally, for about 10 minutes, or until evenly browned. Stir in any remaining marinade with the stock and almonds. Cover the skillet and simmer gently for a further 15 minutes, or until the chicken is completely cooked and tender.

6 Season to taste with a little salt. Garnish the chicken with cilantro and serve immediately with pilau rice, pickles, and poppadums.

Teppanyaki

This simple, Japanese style of cooking is ideal for thinly sliced breast of chicken. Mirin is a rich, sweet rice wine which you can buy in Asian shops, but if it is not available, add one tablespoon of light brown sugar to the sauce instead.

Serves 4
4 boneless chicken breasts
1 red bell pepper
1 green bell pepper
4 scallions
8 baby corn cobs
$1/2$ cup bean sprouts
1 tbsp sesame or sunflower oil
4 tbsp soy sauce
4 tbsp mirin
1 tbsp grated fresh ginger root

1 Remove the skin from the chicken and slice at a slight angle to a thickness of about ¼ inch.

2 Seed and thinly slice the red and green bell peppers, and trim and slice the scallions and corn cobs. Arrange the bell peppers, scallions, corn, and bean sprouts on a plate with the sliced chicken.

3 Heat a large griddle or heavy skillet, then lightly brush with oil. Add the vegetables and chicken slices, in small batches, allowing space between them so that they cook thoroughly.

4 Combine the soy sauce, mirin, and ginger and serve as a dip with the chicken and vegetables.

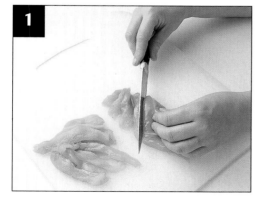

Spanish Chicken with Shrimp

This unusual dish, with its mixture of chicken and shellfish, is typically Spanish.
The basis of this recipe is sofrito—a slow-cooked mixture of onion and tomato in olive oil, with
garlic and bell peppers. Chorizo, a cooked, spicy Spanish sausage, is also used in this recipe.

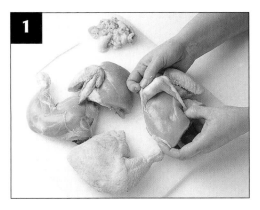

Serves 4
4 chicken quarters
1 tbsp olive oil
1 red bell pepper
1 medium onion
2 garlic cloves, crushed
14 ounce can chopped tomatoes
scant 1 cup dry white wine
4 tbsp chopped fresh oregano
1 cup chorizo sausage
1 cup peeled shrimp
salt and pepper
rice, to serve

1 Remove the skin from the chicken. Heat the oil in a wide, heavy-based skillet and fry the chicken, turning occasionally, until it is golden brown all over.

2 Seed and slice the bell pepper, and peel and slice the onion. Add to the skillet and fry gently to soften.

3 Add the garlic with the tomatoes, wine, and oregano. Season well, then bring to a boil, cover, and simmer gently for 45 minutes, or until the chicken is tender and the juices run clear when the chicken is pierced with the point of a sharp knife.

4 Thinly slice the chorizo and add, together with the shrimp, then simmer for a further 5 minutes. Season to taste with salt and pepper and serve with rice.

Regal Chicken with Cashew Nut Stuffing

Most of the flavorful stuffing is cooked separately from the chicken, only a small amount is added to the neck end.

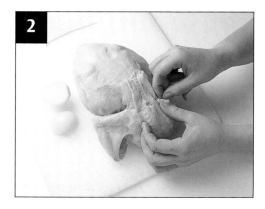

Serves 4
1 chicken, weighing about 3 pounds
1 small onion, halved
2 tbsp butter, melted
1 tsp ground turmeric
1 tsp ground ginger
$1/2$ tsp cayenne
salt and pepper
fresh cilantro, to garnish

STUFFING
2 tbsp oil
1 medium onion, finely chopped
$1/2$ medium red bell pepper, seeded and finely chopped
2 garlic cloves, crushed
$1/2$ cup basmati rice
$1 1/2$ cups hot chicken stock
grated rind of $1/2$ lemon
$1/2$ tsp ground turmeric
$1/2$ tsp ground ginger
$1/2$ tsp ground coriander
pinch cayenne pepper
$1/2$ cup chopped salted cashew nuts
pepper

1 To make the stuffing, heat the oil in a saucepan, add the onion, red bell pepper, and garlic, and cook gently for 4–5 minutes. Add the rice and stir to coat with the oil. Add the stock, bring to a boil, then simmer for 15 minutes, until all the liquid has been absorbed. Transfer to a bowl and add the grated lemon rind, turmeric, ground ginger, ground coriander, cayenne pepper, and cashew nuts. Season to taste with pepper.

2 Place half the stuffing in the neck end of the chicken and secure with a toothpick. Put the halved onion into the cavity of the chicken.

3 Spoon the rest of the rice stuffing into a greased ovenproof dish and cover with foil.

4 Place the chicken in a roasting pan. Prick all over, avoiding the stuffed area. Mix the butter and spices, season with salt and pepper, then brush all over the chicken.

5 Roast in a preheated oven at 375°F for 1 hour, basting from time to time. Place the dish of rice stuffing in the oven and continue to cook the chicken for a further 30 minutes. Remove the toothpick and serve the chicken with the stuffing and gravy.

Mexican Chicken

Chili, tomatoes, and corn are typical ingredients
in a Mexican dish.

Serves 4
2 tbsp oil
8 chicken drumsticks
1 medium onion, finely chopped
1 tsp chili powder
1 tsp ground coriander
14 ounce can chopped tomatoes
2 tbsp tomato paste
$^2/_3$ cup frozen baby corn cobs
salt and pepper
rice and mixed bell pepper salad, to serve

1 Heat the oil in a large skillet, add the chicken drumsticks, and cook over a medium heat until lightly browned all over. Remove from the skillet and set aside.

2 Add the onion to the pan and cook for 3–4 minutes, until soft, then stir in the chili powder and coriander, and cook for a few seconds. Add the chopped tomatoes with their juice and the tomato paste.

3 Return the chicken to the skillet and simmer gently for about 20 minutes until the chicken is tender and thoroughly cooked. Add the corn cobs and cook for a further 3–4 minutes. Season to taste with salt and pepper.

4 Serve with rice and mixed bell pepper salad.

Golden Chicken Pilau

This is a simple version of a creamy textured and mildly spiced Indian pilau. Although there are lots of ingredients, there is very little preparation needed for this dish.

Serves 4
4 tbsp butter
8 skinless, boneless chicken thighs, cut into large pieces
1 medium onion, sliced
1 tsp ground turmeric
1tsp ground cinnamon
1 cup long-grain rice
$1^3/_4$ cups unsweetened yogurt
$1/_3$ cup golden raisins
1 scant cup stock
1 medium tomato, chopped
2 tbsp chopped fresh cilantro or parsley
2 tbsp toasted coconut
salt and pepper
fresh cilantro, to garnish

1 Heat the butter in a heavy-based or nonstick skillet, add the chicken and onion, and fry for about 3 minutes.

2 Stir in the turmeric, cinnamon, rice, and seasoning and fry over a low heat for 3 minutes.

3 Add the yogurt, golden raisins, and stock and mix well. Cover and simmer, stirring occasionally, for 10 minutes, or until the rice is tender and the stock has all been absorbed.

4 Add the tomato and cilantro to the pilau and sprinkle with the toasted coconut. Transfer to a warm serving dish and garnish with fresh cilantro.

Chili Coconut Chicken

This tasty Thai-style dish has a classic sauce of lime, peanut, coconut, and chili.
You will find coconut cream in most supermarkets and delicatessens.

Serves 4
$^1/_3$ cup coconut cream
$^2/_3$ cup hot chicken stock
1 tbsp sunflower oil
8 skinless, boneless chicken thighs, cut into long, thin strips
1 small red chili, thinly sliced
4 scallions, thinly sliced
4 tbsp smooth or crunchy peanut butter
finely grated rind and juice of 1 lime
2 tbsp chopped fresh cilantro (optional)
boiled rice, to serve

1 Dissolve the coconut cream in the chicken stock.

2 Heat the oil in a preheated wok or large heavy-based skillet and fry the chicken, stirring, until golden. Stir in the chili and onions and cook gently for a few minutes.

3 Add the peanut butter, coconut cream, lime rind, and juice and simmer uncovered, stirring, for about 5 minutes. Serve immediately with boiled rice and sprinkle with cilantro, if using.

COOK'S VARIATION

Serve jasmine rice with this spicy dish. It has a fragrant aroma that is well-suited to Thai-style recipes.

Chicken in Red Bell Pepper & Almond Sauce

This tasty chicken dish combines warm spices and almonds
and is spiked with anise.

Serves 4
2 tbsp butter
7 tbsp vegetable oil
4 skinless, boneless chicken breasts, cut into 2 x 1 inch pieces
1 medium onion, roughly chopped
1-inch piece fresh ginger root
3 garlic cloves, peeled
$^1/_4$ cup blanched almonds
1 large red bell pepper, roughly chopped
1 tbsp ground cumin
2 tsp ground coriander
1 tsp ground turmeric
pinch of cayenne pepper
$^1/_2$ tsp salt
$^2/_3$ cup water
3 star anise
2 tbsp lemon juice
pepper

1 Heat the butter and 1 tablespoon of oil in a skillet, add the chicken pieces, and cook, stirring frequently, for 5 minutes, until golden. Transfer the chicken to a plate.

2 Combine the onion, ginger, garlic, almonds, red bell pepper, ground cumin, ground coriander, ground turmeric, cayenne, and salt in a food processor or blender. Process to a smooth paste.

3 Heat the remaining oil in a large saucepan or deep skillet. Add the spice paste and fry, stirring frequently, for 10–12 minutes.

4 Add the chicken pieces, water, star anise, lemon juice, and pepper. Cover, reduce the heat, and simmer gently,

stirring occasionally, for 25 minutes, or until the chicken is tender. Transfer to a warm serving dish and serve.

Caribbean Chicken

This exotic dish can be made with any cut of chicken, but drumsticks are an ideal size for quick and even cooking. Coarsely shredded coconut, or even better, grated fresh coconut, adds a delicious, tropical flavor.

Serves 4
8 skinless chicken drumsticks
2 limes
1 tsp cayenne pepper
2 medium mangoes
1 tbsp sunflower oil
2 tbsp dark brown sugar
2 tbsp coarsely grated coconut (optional), to serve

1 With a sharp knife, slash the chicken drumsticks at intervals, then place the chicken in a large bowl. Grate the rind from the limes and set aside.

2 Squeeze the juice from the limes and sprinkle it over the chicken, together with the cayenne pepper. Cover and chill in the refrigerator for at least two hours or overnight.

3 Peel and slice the mangoes, discarding the pit.

4 Drain the chicken drumsticks, reserving the marinade. Heat the oil in a wide heavy pan and sauté the chicken, turning frequently, until golden. Stir in the reserved marinade, lime rind, mango slices, and the brown sugar.

5 Cover and simmer gently, stirring occasionally, for 15 minutes, or until the juices run clear when the chicken is pierced with the point of a sharp knife. Transfer to a warm serving dish and serve immediately, sprinkled with coconut, if using.

Cajun Chicken Gumbo

This complete main course is cooked in one saucepan for simplicity. If you are cooking for one, simply halve the ingredients; the cooking time should stay the same. The whole chili makes the dish hot and spicy—if you prefer a milder flavor, discard the seeds of the chili.

Serves 2
1 tbsp sunflower oil
4 chicken thighs
1 small onion, diced
2 celery stalks, diced
1 small green bell pepper, diced
$^1/_2$ cup long-grain rice
$1^1/_4$ cups chicken stock
1 small red chili
8 ounces okra
1 tbsp tomato paste
salt and pepper

1 Heat the oil in a wide heavy-based skillet and fry the chicken until golden all over. Remove the chicken from the skillet with a slotted spoon. Stir in the onion, celery, and bell pepper and fry for 1 minute. Pour off any excess fat.

2 Add the rice and fry, stirring, for a further minute. Add the stock and bring to a boil.

3 Thinly slice the chili and trim the okra. Add to the pan with the tomato paste. Season with salt and pepper to taste.

4 Return the chicken to the skillet and stir. Cover tightly and simmer over low heat for 15 minutes, or until the rice is tender, the chicken is thoroughly cooked, and the liquid has been absorbed. Stir occasionally and if it becomes too dry, add a little extra stock to moisten. Serve immediately.

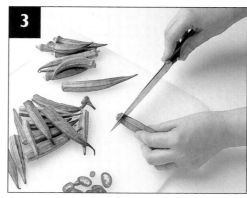

Cumin Spiced Apricot Chicken

Spiced chicken legs are partially boned and packed with dried apricots for an intense fruity flavor.
A golden, spiced, reduced fat yogurt coating keeps the chicken moist and tender.

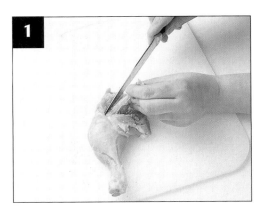

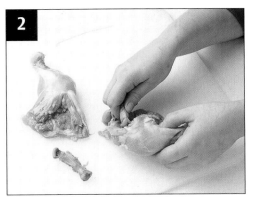

Serves 4
4 large, skinless chicken leg quarters
finely grated rind of 1 lemon
1 cup ready-to-eat dried apricots
1 tbsp ground cumin
1 tsp ground turmeric
1/2 cup reduced fat unsweetened yogurt
salt and pepper

TO SERVE

1 1/2 cups brown rice
2 tbsp slivered hazelnuts or almonds, toasted
2 tbsp sunflower seeds, toasted

1 Remove any excess fat from the chicken legs. Use a small sharp knife to carefully cut the flesh away from the thigh bone.

2 Scrape the meat away down as far as the knuckle. Grasp the thigh bone firmly and twist it to break it away from the drumstick.

3 Open out the boned part of the chicken and sprinkle with lemon rind and pepper. Pack the dried apricots into each piece of chicken.

4 Fold over to enclose, and secure with toothpicks. Mix together the ground cumin, ground turmeric, yogurt, and salt and pepper, then brush this mixture all over the chicken to coat evenly. Place the chicken in an ovenproof dish or

roasting pan and bake in a preheated oven at 375°F for 35–40 minutes, or until the chicken juices run clear, not pink, when pierced through the thickest part with the point of a sharp knife.

5 Meanwhile, cook the rice in boiling, lightly salted water until just tender, then drain well. Stir the hazelnuts and sunflower seeds into the rice and serve with the chicken on a warm serving dish.

Chicken with Bell Peppers & Black Bean Sauce

This tasty chicken stir-fry is quick and easy to make and is full of fresh flavors and crunchy vegetables.

Serves 4
14 ounces chicken breasts, thinly sliced
pinch of cornstarch
2 tbsp oil
1 garlic clove, crushed
1 tbsp black bean sauce
1 each small red and green bell pepper, cut into strips
1 red chili, finely chopped
1 cup mushrooms, sliced
1 onion, chopped
6 scallions, chopped
salt and pepper
noodles

SEASONING
½ tsp salt
½ tsp sugar
3 tbsp chicken stock
1 tbsp dark soy sauce
2 tbsp beef stock
2 tbsp rice wine
1 tsp cornstarch, blended with a little Chinese rice wine

1 Put the chicken strips in a bowl. Add a pinch of salt and a pinch of cornstarch and cover with water. Let stand for 30 minutes.

2 Heat 1 tablespoon of the oil in a wok or deep-sided skillet and stir-fry the chicken for 4 minutes. Remove the chicken to a warm serving dish and clean the wok or skillet.

3 Add the remaining oil to the wok and add the garlic, black bean sauce, green and red bell peppers, chili,

mushrooms, onion, and scallions. Stir-fry for 2 minutes, then return the chicken to the wok.

4 Add the seasoning ingredients, fry for 3 minutes, and thicken with a little cornstarch. Serve with fresh noodles.

COOK'S TIP

Black bean sauce can be found in specialty shops and in many supermarkets. Use dried noodles if you cannot find fresh noodles.

Thai Stir-Fried Chicken with Vegetables

Coconut adds a creamy texture and delicious flavor to this
Thai-style stir-fry, which is spiked with green chili.

Serves 4
3 tbsp sesame oil
12 ounces chicken breasts, thinly sliced
8 shallots, sliced
2 garlic cloves, finely chopped
1–inch piece fresh root ginger, grated
1 green chili, finely chopped
1 red bell pepper, seeded and thinly sliced
1 green bell pepper, seeded and thinly sliced
3 zucchini, thinly sliced
2 tbsp ground almonds
1 tsp ground cinnamon
1 tbsp oyster sauce
$^1/_4$ cup creamed coconut, grated
salt and pepper

1 Heat the sesame oil in a preheated wok, add the chicken, season to taste with salt and pepper, and stir fry for about 4 minutes.

2 Add the shallots, garlic, ginger, and chili to the wok and stir-fry for 2 minutes.

3 Add the bell peppers and zucchini and cook for about 1 minute.

4 Finally, add the ground almonds, cinnamon, oyster sauce, and coconut. Stir fry for 1 minute. Transfer the stir-fry to a warm serving dish and serve immediately.

Chicken Korma

Korma is a typically mild and aromatic curry. If you want to reduce the fat in this recipe, use unsweetened yogurt instead of the cream.

Serves 4–6
1 1/2 pounds chicken meat, cut into cubes
1 1/4 cups heavy cream
1/2 tsp garam masala
rice, to serve

KORMA PASTE
2 garlic cloves
1-inch fresh ginger root, coarsely chopped
1/3 cup blanched almonds
6 tbsp chicken stock
1 tsp ground cardamom
4 cloves, crushed
1 tsp cinnamon
2 large onions, chopped
1 tsp coriander seeds
2 tsp ground cumin seeds
pinch cayenne
6 tbsp olive oil
salt and pepper
cilantro, to garnish

1 Place all the ingredients for the korma paste into a blender or food processor and process until a very smooth paste is formed.

2 Coat the chicken with the korma paste and chill for 3 hours. Simmer the meat in a large saucepan, adding a little chicken stock if dry.

3 Simmer for 25 minutes, add the cream and garam masala, and simmer for a further 15 minutes. Allow the korma to stand for 10 minutes. Transfer to a warm serving dish and garnish with cilantro. Serve with rice.

Fruity Garlic Curried Chicken

Serve this fruity curry with mango chutney and nan bread, and top the curry with seedless grapes. Mango or pears make a good substitute for pineapple.

Serves 4–6
1 tbsp oil
1³/₄ pounds chicken meat, chopped
4 tbsp flour, seasoned
1 pound shallots, roughly chopped
4 garlic cloves, crushed with a little olive oil
3 cooking apples, diced
1 pineapple, diced
³/₄ cup golden raisins
1 tbsp clear honey
1¹/₄ cups chicken stock
2 tbsp Worcestershire sauce
3 tbsp hot curry paste
²/₃ cup sour cream
salt and pepper
rice to serve

1 Heat the oil in a large skillet. Coat the meat in the seasoned flour and cook for about 4 minutes, until it is browned all over. Transfer the chicken to a large deep casserole.

2 Sauté the shallots, garlic, apples, pineapple, and golden raisins in the skillet juices over a low heat.

3 Add the chicken stock, seasoning, Worcestershire sauce, and curry paste.

4 Pour the sauce over the chicken and cover the casserole with a lid or cooking foil.

5 Cook in the center of a preheated oven at 350°F for 2 hours. Stir in the sour cream and cook for a further 15 minutes. Serve with rice.

Index

Index compiled by Hilary Bird.